Computer Environments for Children

Computer Environments for Children
A Reflection on Theories of Learning and Education

Cynthia Solomon

The MIT Press
Cambridge, Massachusetts
London, England

This book was set in Times Roman by E/F Typographic Lab and printed and bound by The Murray Printing Co. in the United States of America.

Library of Congress Cataloging-in-Publication Data

132090

Solomon, Cynthia.
  Computer environments for children.

  Originally presented as the author's thesis
(doctoral—Harvard University, 1985).
  Bibliography: p.
  Includes index.
  1. Mathematics—Computer-assisted instruction.
2. Computer-assisted instruction. 3. Mathematics
—Study and teaching (Elementary) I. Title.
QA20.C65S64 1986   372.13'9445   86-3018
ISBN 0-262-19249-7

Contents

Acknowledgments

The ideas for this book grew out of my research on the uses of computers in education. Many people have helped, guided, and taught me. I mention only a few here by name, but I would like to express my gratitude to all the children and adults with whom I worked over the years. Even so, I might not have finished the book if I had not taken time to pursue a doctorate in education at Harvard University. I wrote a preliminary paper in 1980. Finally, in the spring of 1985, I carried it further and turned it into a doctoral thesis. Don Oliver, Seymour Papert, and Sheldon (Shep) White, my thesis advisors, were invaluable in helping me shape the material. I am indebted to Seymour for his vision, his brilliant insights, his patience, and his ability to translate succinctly complex ideas into understandable statements. He has had a profound influence on my intellectual development for the past twenty years. In balance, and especially when I could not say what I wanted, Shep came to my aid as a sympathetic listener and sharp critic offering another point of view. Shep has been generous with his time and comments.

In the early phases of this work, I spent many hours with Mimi Sinclair discussing the roles that computers might play in children's lives and the theoretical roots influencing those roles. In a later phase, I took to making lengthy long-distance phone calls to Brian Harvey in California. Brian's comments were always evocative, important, and rewarding, as were the many hours of discussion we had on the state of computers in education. In the final stages of editing and transforming a doctoral thesis into a publishable book, I got invaluable help from Hal Abelson as well as from Brian. Hal was amazing; his penetrating, softly worded comments resulted in a month of revisions. Ricky Carter's critique was also helpful, and Bruce Ehrmann's editorial assistance greatly improved the manuscript. Phil Apley was wonderful to me; he kept my computer running and calmly responded to a few frantic emergency calls. Gail Farrish, Clyde Lewis, and their mother, my Aunt Bea, encouraged me to continue at times when I was ready to give up.

Other friends and colleagues who have fundamentally influenced my thinking about computers and people include Margaret Minsky, Gary Drescher, Marvin Minsky, Alan Kay, Greg Gargarian, Howard Austin, and my nephews, Erric and Jon Solomon. All the members of the MIT Logo Group during the 1970s and the Apple Logo team at Logo Computer Systems, Inc. in the early 1980s helped shape my ideas about computers. An important influence for me was the twenty month experience as director of Atari Cambridge Research (1982–1984). We tried to move toward a future in which children would communicate, through finger touch and body movement, with a computer that had not only high-resolution color graphics capable of real-time animation but also an intelligent music system for performance, composition, and exploration, as well as a powerful programming environment that, in a sense, modernized Logo. At the same time, we were helping to debug Logo for the Atari 800 computer and prepare demonstration material. Although this book does not discuss the Atari experience, mixing the past and future into a twenty month presence had a positive effect on the book.

Finally, I give special thanks to Pat Suppes, Bob Davis, Tom Dwyer, and Seymour Papert.

1

Computers in Education

Not long ago, the idea of a computer connected to a television set in your own home seemed a science fiction fantasy. By the 1980s the situation had changed. Although many people have not used computers personally, their image of computers in homes and offices is no longer one of science fiction. Microelectronics, the technology of the 1970s, brought computers out of the laboratory and into our everyday lives. The computer's presence offers a new opportunity to improve the quality of education. At the same time it has created a new educational challenge that emerges when we ask how people learn to use these machines and what computing environments are available to them.

For educators, a nagging question is, How do I learn to use computers today in a way that will not be obsolete in five years? The answer requires a vision of the future. But how can we develop a vision of the future? Journalists and businessmen might try to build their vision of the future by projecting statistics on how many computers schools are using today. Alas, school administrators often follow their example. To project to the future we need to understand more deeply what happened in the past. In this book I take a close look at the development of educational computing not by counting computers but by examining the underlying theoretical issues. These issues do not fall solely in one domain but span across the traditional concerns of philosophers, psychologists, educators, and computer scientists. In fact, the new computer educator emerges as one with a foundation in each of these disciplines.

In discussing the development of educational computing, I concentrate on innovative uses of computers in elementary mathematics education stemming from research in the 1960s and 1970s. Much of the research of those decades laid the groundwork for current thought. But educational innovations carry with them a continuing concern in education—the problem of transmitting theory into practice. The process of transmission often contributes to the trivialization of the educational innovation.

The gap in communication between the new intellectual tradition of computing and its practice is amplified by the microcomputer. Discussions begin again: Will the new technology dramatically transform the way education takes place? At the same time, computers are entering schools; but, although the computer and ideas to support innovative uses are present, there is a lag in educators' understanding of computers and how they relate to learning and thinking. Again the problem is an educational one: What do educational computerists need to know, and how can they acquire this knowledge?

Although we know that acquiring new knowledge takes time and personal involvement, we rarely display this understanding when we create opportunities for teachers to explore new avenues of learning; and we often misjudge new areas of knowledge for extensions of previously acquired knowledge. Consequently, teachers are given piecemeal workshops and courses in which to "survey" new subject areas.

The Problem

Educators might agree that the computer's presence offers a new opportunity to enhance children's lives and to improve the quality, content, and delivery of education. They might agree that the computer can be an intellectual tool for both learner and teacher. Nonetheless, whether we will see this qualitative improvement depends on how much educators take advantage of the computer's potential. Doing so requires an understanding of what is possible.

Educators might question where to use computers, what computers to buy, what software to buy, or what new hardware and software are needed. In schools, further questions might include how many computers are needed and where are teachers with computer expertise? These questions can be answered in different ways. For instance, the answers might be: Use the computers in classrooms; buy Apples; get printers, touch tablets, color monitors; get Logo, a word processing package, assorted games. And give every child a computer; hire a computer specialist; and retrain some of the staff. These answers have profound ramifications, not the least of which is that they obscure far deeper issues.

Contrasting Images in Current Practice

Because more teachers have become involved with computers, a growing tendency has emerged: introducing children to computers by exposing them to various educational software packages, including games, and to word processing, BASIC programming, and Logo programming with turtle graphics. This exposure approach trivializes intellectual pursuits that cannot be completed in five or ten minutes. This approach is encouraged by school computing facilities, where not only do the teachers lack experience and time to gain expertise but also a few microcomputers must be shared with thirty or more children.

Curriculum planning guidelines often fail to express what children might want to know to help them in their learning and development. Typically, curriculum planners see four categories of activities: computer literacy, programming, games, and computer-assisted instruction. They then begin to detail this practice. Computer literacy, to illustrate just one of the categories, assumes many different guises. Primarily, children are asked to be aware of what the computer's components are, what the computer can do and what its limitations are, as well as various social implications. These are hard questions that deserve deep thought and reflection; the children's answers change with personal experience in using the computer. This kind of course, especially in quick and isolated exposures, can be misleading and may further trivialize the computer's potential as a learning instrument.

Something quite different might happen in a computer studies course that meets three or four periods a week. Something even more dramatic might happen when children can tap the computer's potential at any time. Computing experiences might offer children another way to examine issues that arise in their daily lives.

For example, the following experience is typical of the kind of observations I have made of children in Logo classes over the years (Papert and Solomon 1970a; Papert 1971b). A class of seventh graders had been developing programs to teach themselves algebra. They were working on programs to generate simple linear equations. Then they used these programs and were amazed that they could indeed solve such equations. Some students developed special drill programs to help them in multiplication. Others developed teaching programs for younger children. In the process, they faced several issues and were struck in different ways by the computer responses they themselves had built. Some of the error messages had been jeers they commonly heard in school, such as "Dummy, go back to first grade!" These remarks were not helpful to them. They began to think about how the program could be more helpful. They wondered when to give the correct answer. They thought about whether to provide remediation in the form of simpler problems. Then they had to think about what simpler problems might be. This led to class discussions about teaching strategies and learning. They wondered if flash card techniques were the best way to learn. They began to talk about where and when they used computations of this sort in their everyday lives. In these activities, the children were aware of the joys of a creative process in which they designed and implemented learning environments. Simultaneously, the children were confronted with issues about sharing information, adapting other people's ideas, copying other people's work, giving appropriate credit. They also had to deal with broken computers or their own carelessness resulting in lost work; they had to worry about the allocation of computer resources as well. With microcomputers the children had additional concerns about lost, stolen, or damaged diskettes and whether to replicate copy-protected material. When the issues were of immediate concern, the discussions resulted in adjusting the rules of social behavior with regard to computing activities.

The scope of activities within the computing experience of these children ranged from learning the particular skills of solving simple linear equations, multiplying, and designing, implementing, and debugging programs to becoming aware of different learning styles and facing social issues caused by the computer's presence. All were grounded in the children's own experiences and needs. In my work with other groups of children, the particular skills or social and psychological issues under discussion have varied, but a similar sense of self-awareness and intellectual stance has emerged.

Responding to the Problem

In the 1960s and 1970s, several research laboratories in universities and industry offered models of how computers might contribute to the learning process. Four exemplars are discussed in this book. They range from behaviorist models of learning (in which the students are guided every step of the way) to Piagetian and other developmental models (in which the students are encouraged to develop their own paths toward learning). These research activities have been foundational to current trends in schools, although many practitioners are unaware of this intellectual history, and thus, the influence of this research has been impressionistic rather than structural.

Narrowing my examination to four researchers created the challenge and difficulty of selection. Ultimately, each exponent represents a different stream of thinking within education. Each has strong theoretical convictions that have been put into practice. And the work of each illustrates the profound influence computers—and ideas born from thinking about computers—have on those who use them. Furthermore, each is a colleague and friend, whose work I know and respect.

As a first strategy in exploring the many ways computers have been used in education, I focus on two images of the computer: (1) the computer as an interactive textbook in control of the user and (2) the computer as an expressive medium under the control of the user. As examples of the computer-as-textbook, I chose two different approaches. Patrick Suppes, of Stanford University, developed a system to provide students with sequenced drill-and-practice exercises, whereas Robert Davis, of the University of Illinois, using the Plato system, imbued the computer with a Socratic style of interaction. With regard to the computer as expressive medium, I again chose two approaches. Tom Dwyer and his colleagues at the Soloworks laboratory at the University of Pittsburgh developed a variety of programming activities around BASIC, and Seymour Papert and his Logo group at the Massachusetts Institute of Technology developed new mathematics and new technology for children.

Another strategy of this book is to treat each trend in terms of its relationship to elementary school education and to concentrate on examples from work in mathematics. I selected elementary education because my own interests have crystallized around children, their social, intellectual, and emotional development, and how teachers can contribute to the developmental process. I chose mathematics because the methods of computer usage in this area represent general theories of instruction and epistemological positions that take on different forms in different disciplines but happen to be most clearly realized in mathematics.

Developing a Personal Computational View

I approached these studies from the perspective that computers can be personal learning instruments for *everyone*. From this vantage, I think it is important for people, whether they are designers of environments or participants in the environments, to think about the role they play and the explicit and implicit assumptions they make within their environment. This kind of awareness is what I take as literacy, whether in computing, reading, or writing: to be aware that each environment or system carries with it many underlying assumptions and to be aware of one's own role and assumptions within the environment.

For me, therefore, *literacy* means more than being able to read and write; the word refers to an intellectual stance. In this book I imply an extension of the term *literacy* to the world of computers. It presents some of the intellectual fruits of exploring ideas related to computation in ways not unlike the methods that literate people generally use to explore and relate ideas. I do not attempt to catalog *all* the knowledge about computers a person may have or need. What I do here is explore an example, a model, an illustration of a method of approach. I take some ideas about computers and try to locate them in a literate fashion—to understand their origins, to place them in a context, to examine their intellectual traditions and their relationship to the development of new ideas.

Educational Computing before Microcomputers

The emergence of time-sharing in the 1960s sparked high hopes for the use of computers in education and led to the investment of large sums of money in a movement that fizzled dramatically. Time-shared computing was the prevailing technology in the 1960s. It was a step toward personal computing. The goal of time-sharing was to bring people into immediate and intimate contact with *computing*. Although the key to time-sharing was the *sharing* of the computer among as large a community of users as possible, the user was to *feel* a direct and personal relationship with the machine. Typewriter terminals replaced punched cards as the standard mode of communication between human and machine. Feedback from the computer was presented in seconds rather than in hours or days. Previously, communication between person and machine was transacted through "batch processing," whereby prepared programs were submitted to the computer and much later the computer's responses were delivered to the user as a printout.

The hope was that, through sharing the computer's resources among many users, the cost of computing would become small enough so that by the 1980s everyone would have easy access to computers. The work of the 1960s was directed toward harnessing the computer—in its time-shared capacity—to serve many people as quickly as possible.

The demand for immediate products and large-scale effects relegated the dominant use of computers, in that decade, to computer assisted instruction (CAI) and introductory programming in the BASIC language. CAI sessions could be brief and timed and did not eat up the computer's memory. On the other hand, programming was more time consuming and demanding of computer memory. BASIC, compared with other languages such as FORTRAN, did not demand a lot of computer memory (Kemeny and Kurtz 1985, p. 57).

At all levels of education, including college, BASIC and CAI were greeted warmly. But by the mid-1970s, the educational promise of BASIC and CAI began to fade. University computer science programs chose structured and procedural languages such as Pascal or LISP, as carriers of computational ideas. This adoption is reflected in the current trend of high schools to teach Pascal. Logo is replacing BASIC as the language taught in elementary schools.

The difficulties of teachers actually writing course materials led to a growing disappointment with CAI systems in the 1970s: Quality courseware was not easy to generate in them. Telling the computer about subject matter, the variability of students' learning styles, and the problem of how to tutor students quickly became insoluble issues. Researchers began to raise other areas of concern, anticipating the development of intelligent CAI (Brown 1977; Burton and Brown 1978). The educational computer movement based on time-sharing lost its momentum. A new movement based on personal computers was being anticipated in research settings but was not yet a reality in schools. Thus Alan Kay, then a Xerox researcher, envisioned a personal computer with which people could write, edit, and illustrate papers and also devise new learning environments (Kay 1977; Nace 1984).

For Kay, the

protean nature of the computer is such that it can act like a machine or like a language to be shaped and exploited. It is a medium that can dynamically simulate the details of any other medium, including media that cannot exist physically. It is not a tool, although it can act like many tools. It is the first metamedium, and as such it has degrees of freedom for representation and expression never before encountered and as yet barely investigated. Even more important, it is fun, and therefore intrinsically worth doing. (Kay 1984, p. 59)

This vision, born in the 1970s, is likely to have a major impact on elementary education in the 1990s.

In the meantime, by the mid-1970s, the microcomputer became a reality, calling for a reexamination of computers. The microcomputer can be seen in two ways: as a thing in itself, a primitive thing that actually inhibits exciting, progressive thinking in the rush to get a computer next Monday; or as a harbinger of great computer power at low cost and a stimulus to exciting research.

Time-sharing, as envisioned in its formative years, is surely dead. But serious thinking had been embedded in its uses. The theoretical ideas developed in that period, as we will see, are surely not dead. Digesting them will prepare us for the next period, when the word *protean* frequently used by "visionaries" such as Kay and Seymour Papert, becomes a true description of the machines to which children have access.

Studying Computers in Education

A considerable body of literature has arisen concerning uses of computers in education. The literature has typically been problem oriented and *ad hoc*. Both individual research papers and multi-million-dollar funded projects generally address computer effectiveness in a particular situation; they set out to prove that this or that program or approach is expedient. This book takes a more structured survey of educational uses of computers. Its guiding idea is to see current practices in terms of intellectual traditions in the philosophy of education, in theories of psychology and even in the foundations of subject matter being taught—such as mathematics. I adopt the strategy of discussing an individual or a team, in each case considering the intellectual origins, the approach to using the computer, and the extent to which this approach has penetrated school practice and been evaluated. What follows is an overview of each proponent's positions on mathematics, instruction, and learning. The details are discussed in the next four chapters.

Computer as Interactive Textbook

Suppes: Drill and Practice and Rote Learning

Patrick Suppes, a professor at Stanford University with appointments in the psychology, philosophy and other departments, is director of the Institute for Mathematical Studies in the Social Sciences. He is also president of Computer Curriculum Corporation (CCC), which produces and markets his computer-based educational materials. The institute is the laboratory where Suppes conducted most of his computer research.

Suppes comes to computers from a background in philosophy and logic. He has a logical approach to mathematics and a behavioristic, mathematical modeling theory of learning: Mathematics—or any other subject matter—can be broken down into individual facts; the relationship among the individual facts or elements can be organized hierarchically. In this analysis subject matter is composed of local knowledge: One fact leads to another fact that exists higher in the logical structure.

Teaching children this body of information involves presenting them with exercises (stimuli) and reinforcing their responses. Reinforcement consists of structuring the following responses: Telling the children they are "correct" and presenting a new exercise, telling them they are "wrong" and re-presenting the exercise, or telling them they are wrong, telling them the correct response, and then re-presenting the exercise. The teacher's job (assumed by the computer) is to present increasingly harder exercises, each building on the previous experience of the children and leading finally to knowing the specified body of information.

Computers are particularly attractive to Suppes because they deliver exercises to different children in the same teaching styles; and yet computers can be programmed to individualize the content by selecting easier or harder exercises, depending on how the student has performed in the past. The computer can act as a psychologist and collect empirical data on children's behavior. Predictive performance models can be developed and tested on actual data. This in turn can lead to programs that can better individualize the instructional path.

Suppes's elementary mathematics curriculum is available on CCC systems. This drill-and-practice approach has great appeal to school districts with large populations of students who are not performing at grade level and need remediation. Suppes's own analyses of computational skills have shown that the computer does as well in five to ten minutes per student session per day as a good teacher doing the same sort of drill and practice in 25-minute sessions per day (Suppes and Morningstar 1969), at least for poor and minority students.

In 1976, the Los Angeles Unified School District and the Educational Testing Service, under a grant from the National Institutes of Education, began a four-year study of CCC's curriculum effectiveness in elementary mathematics, reading, and language arts on fourth- through sixth-grade students (Ragosta et al. 1982). The children received ten or twenty minutes of computer instruction per day. The results show significant improvement in the computational skills test scores of the children studied. The evaluation of the reading and language arts components shows that test scores did not significantly improve; however, the children's scores did not decrease over the period of the study either.

This "rote learning" approach to education has strong support in educational practice. It also plays on the popular hopes that machines can teach skills with which teachers have been unsuccessful, to populations with which school systems have been unsuccessful. Both the rote learning approaches to educational uses of computers and the computer as intelligent, sympathetic teacher have strong support from industry and government.

Davis: Socratic Interactions and Discovery Learning
Robert B. Davis is a mathematics educator, a teacher of teachers and children, and a developer of "new math" curricula for elementary school-children. He is one of several mathematicians and scientists who began to reappraise the postwar conditions of elementary education in light of such scientific developments as Sputnik. Davis saw many problems in elementary mathematics classrooms of the 1950s, in particular, that arithmetic was being taught without relating it to its use in, for example, algebra, geometry, or science and that rote learning styles of teaching were not conducive to real learning (Davis 1964, 1967). Thus Davis differs from Suppes in at least two respects. For Davis, mathematics is seen through a pragmatic rather than a logical prism, and the mechanism of learning is seen as discovery rather than repetitive reinforcement.

Davis set out to embed the learning of arithmetic in a richer context and at the same time began a campaign to change the classroom atmosphere and the dominant teaching style. He shared with other innovators the belief that children learn best informally and through discovering for themselves. Psychologically this theory received support from Jean Piaget's research in Switzerland. For Davis, Piaget's work suggested new routes to understanding children's mathematical thinking and provided a context for apprehending these issues. Davis has been particularly attracted by the computational models of thinking suggested by artificial intelligence researchers (Davis 1973; Minsky and Papert 1972; Minsky 1975; Newell and Simon 1972; Papert 1980a; Brown 1977). The cognitive sciences, using computational metaphors and techniques, have provided further insights into mathematical thinking and ways of talking about children's misconceptions.

Davis's teaching strategy was to draw on children's everyday experiences. His paradigmatic teaching strategy would look for examples, such as children sharing a candy bar with friends, as a way of introducing formal mathematics. Using another tactic, he would challenge children to figure out new mathematical relationships through a Socratic dialogue (Davis 1964b, 1967). Davis evolved his own math materials and adapted others and was an advocate of using manipulative materials, such as Dienes blocks, in elementary classrooms (Davis 1984).

A part of Davis's philosophy of education is to create activities in the math classroom that children can do as mathematicians would. Two important elements of being a mathematician are making discoveries and especially making generalizations. These activities occur in a specific body of knowledge, consisting of basic arithmetic facts and techniques, within the context of algebra, coordinate geometry, graphing functions, etc. Thus, when Davis began to implement an elementary mathematics curriculum in a computer environment, he had in mind a definite curriculum and a definite style of teaching, as well as a model of a child.

Davis began his work on the Plato system as part of an evaluation project, in which elementary mathematics served as one indicator of the system's success as an instructional medium. He started in the fall of 1972, developing materials for grades 4 through 6, and was evaluated by the Educational Testing Service (ETS) in 1974. ETS found his project —although not all the Plato curricula—effective (Alderman et al. 1978; Amarel 1978).

The delivery, the content, and the computer system itself are different from the CCC system. In contrast to Suppes's learning environment, Davis's places great importance on graphics and visual representations as integrated components in the formulation of material. In chapters 2 and 3 I give a picture of these different curricula.

Computer as Expressive Medium

Dwyer: Eclecticism and Heuristic Learning

Tom Dwyer has an eclectic confidence that creating conditions favorable to exploration will lead to discovery and effective learning. The computer offers an opportunity to create such conditions. Unlike Suppes or Davis, Dwyer does not proceed from elaborated theories of psychology or of mathematics. Before joining the computer science faculty at the University of Pittsburgh, Dwyer taught science and mathematics in high school. His emphasis is on the practical work of finding activities in which the child can use the computer as a personal tool. Teachers are important in this process.

Teacher and student become...co-discoverers of truths. The methods they learn to use, and the results they obtain, display a freshness that suggests that they have personally discovered a secret that transcends the art of any one great teacher. Their secret, put simply, is to use computer technology to build an environment in which learning mathematics is both natural and exciting. (Dwyer 1975)

The guiding principle of Dwyer's educational thinking is expressed in a metaphor drawn from his own experiences as an airplane pilot. The critical goal of the early phase of teaching someone to fly an airplane is bringing the student to the point at which she can "solo." If the student can take over and put herself in a position of soloing, then she can learn to fly by flying. Dwyer sees the importance of the computer as allowing students to engage in solo learning. Thus they can attain much earlier a position in which they are not dependent on the teacher or on the curriculum to direct them in successive steps.

The problem then is to build an educational setting that supports creative solo learning while simultaneously addressing the importance of a standard repertoire. Teacher-student controlled computing provides exactly such a setting. (Dwyer 1975, p. 77)

The computer becomes a personal tool that stretches into many different areas and provides different experiences, for example, "computer experience in the manner of artistic creation, and computer experience for acquiring specific knowledge" (Critchfield 1979, p. 18). Furthermore, these experiences might come from programming the computer or from running a program on the computer.

Dwyer sees the computer as an expressive medium and as a source of inspiration to teachers and students. He is also a firm believer in working with the tools at hand. By choosing the computing facilities that were most readily available, he used the BASIC programming language first on time-shared computers and then on home computers. His approach builds on the enthusiasm and imagination of teachers. Because BASIC has been the most popular language of microcomputers, imaginative teachers have found Dwyer's Soloworks materials and his books on BASIC helpful.

Unlike the other approaches, Dwyer's has not been the subject of exhaustive evaluation. Its eclectic nature has led to adaptation in math and science classes primarily as an adjunct learning activity. His approach lends itself to popular beliefs that learning to program is a social requirement for an educated person and a preparation for the work world. Therefore Dwyer's work is frequently translated into learning the rudiments of a computer language, such as BASIC. It is often introduced to children by teachers who lack foundation in programming and in applying computational ideas to children's learning. The emphasis is on language development skills. Dwyer himself emphasized process, the process of being deeply involved in engaging programming activities. This process is linked to a rather eclectic approach to how learning takes place and what children learn.

Papert: Constructivism and Piagetian Learning
For Seymour Papert, learning best occurs in an active environment, in which children participate in the process by constructing objects. The concept of solo learning is again a central idea, with students embarking on self-chosen and self-directed projects.

Papert adheres to a concrete philosophy of education and a definite epistemology of subject matter; both drawn in part from Piaget and artificial intelligence. Papert's background is in computer science, mathematics, philosophy, and psychology. He was a close collaborator of Piaget before designing Logo. He has a deep interest in mechanisms of mind—in trying to understand how people learn, how to make machines intelligent, and how one might contribute to knowledge about the other. Papert's conception of mathematics is broad and includes learning to get around one's environment, solving problems in clever ways, using one's intuition, and reflecting on one's actions. Doing mathematics consists, in part, of constructing objects—both mental and physical—and debugging them. Papert's goal continues to be the evolution of a ''mathland,'' a mathematical world that children can explore freely and comprehend by inventing, constructing, and using computational entities.

Logo is one such example. It has become synonymous with a way of thinking about computers and about learning. It is a computer language created by Papert for children, and it has also become a computational environment including a set of computer-controllable devices, such as floor turtles, music boxes, and graphics turtles. Because the environment is rich in content, teachers' roles are changed. In fact, the curriculum is developed by the children's own explorations. Like the children, teachers also make discoveries about themselves, about their students, and about the mathland they are exploring. The likelihood of children learning the basic facts and techniques that Suppes and Davis value is high. These are tools the children acquire facility with in their explorations. For Papert knowing a collection of facts, or having skills at summoning up those facts, is not being a mathematician. Knowing how to obtain those facts if and when they are needed is being a mathematician.

Papert's work has also undergone evaluation at the behest of the National Science Foundation. The evaluation, as with the other evaluations indicated that this approach is effective. Several other studies have been undertaken (Pea 1983, 1984; Higginson 1984). The Pea study involved two experimental classrooms at the Bank Street College School in New York. It tried to measure the transfer of planning skills from Logo to other areas. The task chosen for this evaluation was asking children who had been in a Logo class to describe how they would clean their room. Not so surprisingly, they did not seem to plan that task very well. The Higginson study involved looking at several different classrooms in several different schools in which the teachers were not given much prior training in how to use computers in their classroom. The findings of this study indicate that interesting things occur in classes with good teachers.

Logo became available on the Apple II and other microcomputers in 1982. Since then, Logo has been heralded as the programming language of choice for elementary school students, whereas BASIC has been regarded increasingly as appropriate for junior high school students. But Logo as mathland has not yet happened. Papert has set its direction, but more research and development are needed. Its method is perhaps the most difficult to adopt because it suggests a radically different way of thinking about children and school curricula.

Concluding Remarks

Building educational computing environments and learning and teaching with them are three activities that can come together in different ways and give rise to different computer cultures. That is, the way people and computers inform one another influences the way people think about, talk about, and use computers. That different computer environments give rise to different computer cultures is in itself important. But children and teachers who are learning to use computers need to develop an awareness of different computer cultures, and they must blend these cultures to create their own.

The way in which a child communicates with the computer and what child and computer talk about are essential to these learning environments. The environments are man-made, so they represent one person's or group's views of the very entelechy of how people interact with one another and with machines. For example, when computers are used as "teaching machines" that control student interaction, assumptions are being made about the child, the content, and the computer's role. These assumptions and the range of approaches that computers might be programmed to assume are intellectual issues that are powerful elements in developing an understanding of computers in education.

When children learn to control computers, they construct programs and in the process often invent different methods to achieve a particular effect. These different methods frequently lead to thinking about other problems. Thus computer environments can offer children opportunities to develop their intellectual abilities by making personal discoveries through a continuous process of building on what they already know. Children can gain concrete experience with dynamic processes acting separately or together, one at a time or in parallel. Debugging or enacting these processes is itself an ongoing process involving personal styles and values. It also involves an outside criterion of whether the computer is behaving as expected. Computers provide a reaffirmation of the idea that knowledge and understanding are more than a discrete collection of facts.

The focus of this book can now be restated as a discussion of the concepts underpinning the uses of computers in education, with a view to giving a picture of what computer literacy means in different contexts. I discuss innovative research of the 1960s and 1970s in order to shed light on today's practices. A problem for the future is that it is becoming harder to find laboratories that are *now* looking at these issues in light of further advances in computational ideas. One might argue that this hiatus gives society as a whole time to catch up, digest, learn, and form intelligent opinions about the role of computers. But building systems and testing and debugging new theories take time. Long-term research is needed for the next generation of computer-enhanced learning environments. The need to reassess ideas developed earlier and to examine how these ideas are introduced into classrooms exists *now*.

Educational computing has become a multi-million dollar business. Much of the software now available takes its ideas from the research discussed in this book. Its transformed state, however, is not usually researched. Often, software is thrust onto the market without adequate research; nevertheless it attains popularity. This tendency for educational software to become successful without research makes research in this area more difficult. One piece of software can make or break a company; its success or lack of success may have little to do with the research behind it. This limited but lucrative approach to education contributes to the difficulties of pursuing and obtaining educational research support, especially since research and development of new ideas applied to hardware and software take time and money—perhaps a research and development cycle of about ten years. Linking what is being currently developed for the marketplace with what might be developed in the future as computers become cheaper, smaller, more powerful, and more interesting might require strong ties between university researchers and industry. Important investigative questions for educators remain: What is the potential role of computers in education? How can teachers use computers now? And how will the computer change the content and context of schooling?

My intention here is to offer a context in which to explore these questions. My goals are to provide a foundation for serious discussion about educational uses of computers, to suggest some images for future computer research, and to suggest one possible route into computing for educators.

2

Suppes: Drill and Practice and Rote Learning

The computer, when used in education, has a way of exaggerating differences: Behaviorist educators become more behaviorist, and proponents of open education come to espouse greater degrees of freedom. A closer look at how Suppes uses the computer to create learning environments brings out in sharp relief some features and problems of the behaviorist approach to education. In this chapter a brief description of the elementary mathematics curriculum is given, followed by a discussion of the attractive features of this kind of learning environment, including a discussion on the evaluation and economics of such learning environments. The concluding remarks focus on the weaknesses and paradoxes of this kind of learning environment.

Description of an Arithmetic Curriculum

The best description of this concrete approach is through a concrete example. Behaviorism tends to favor fragmentation of knowledge into small units, and elementary school arithmetic lends itself to such an approach. The Suppes curriculum is an example of such fragmentation. It is divided into units whose nature has evolved over the course of time. Initially the units were blocks, each designed around a "concept." From 1965 to 1966 the fourth-grade curriculum was to have forty-one concept blocks. By 1969 each grade level consisted of from twenty to twenty-seven concept blocks. Each concept block was made up of five sets of exercises at different levels of difficulty. As an example of level of difficulty, the following exercises were taken from the concept block "sums 0–40 intended for the fourth grade" (Suppes, Jerman, and Brian 1968, pp. 206–210):

Level 2: $24 + \underline{} = 24$
$24 + 3 = \underline{}$ sums 0–30
$\underline{} + 2 = 25$

Level 3: $26 + \_\_ = 29$
$40 + 0 = \_\_$ sums 0–40
$\_\_ + 4 = 38$

Level 4: $0 + 29 = 0 + \_\_$
$22 + 7 = \_\_ + 142$ terms on either side of equal sign
$33 + 1 = 7 + \_\_$

Level 5: $(20 + 1) + 8 = 24 + \_\_$
$(4 + 16) + 8 = \_\_ + 22$
$(14 + 11) + 2 = 18 + \_\_$

By 1969 a concept block was standardly covered in seven sessions (days). "Each concept block included a preliminary test (or pretest), 5 days of drill, a subsequent test (or posttest), and sets of review drills and review posttests" (Suppes and Morningstar 1969, p. 343). "The tests and drills presented to the student for the 7 days required for each concept block were as follows. Day 1, pretest; day 2 to 5, drill and review drill; day 6, drill and review posttest; day 7, posttest" (Suppes and Morningstar 1969, p. 344).

The level of difficulty of the drills is determined by the student's performance on the tests and drills. If a student gets more than 80% correct on a drill or test, then he goes up a level. If he gets less than 60% correct, he goes down a level; and if he gets between 60 and 80% correct, he stays at the same level. The posttest is made up of exercises from previous concept blocks the student has encountered as well as from the one he is currently finishing. The review drills are at a constant level of difficulty and are selected from a previous concept block, one for which the student's posttest score was lowest. His review posttest score replaces the former posttest score. The student does not receive the same review drill two weeks in a row despite his score.

Another significant change occurred in the history of this learning environment. The entire elementary mathematics curriculum for grades 1 through 6 was recategorized into fourteen concept areas or "strands." Each strand is divided into five to ten equivalence classes within a grade level. A student can thus progress a tenth of a grade level at a time. The strands are given in table 2.1 (Suppes, Searle, Kanz, and Martin Clinton 1972 (revised 1977), p. 4). The areas of mathematics explicitly left out of the curriculum at that time were geometry and word problems. Researchers at Suppes's Institute for Mathematical Studies in the Social Sciences (IMSSS) had conducted exploratory work in these areas and found that these areas needed more computer memory and time than was economically feasible at that time.

By 1984, CCC prepared a new release of the elementary mathematics curriculum that recategorized the material for grades 1 through 7 into twelve strands: addition, number concepts, U.S. measurement, subtraction, equa-

Table 2.1
Description of strands

Strand	Name	Abbreviation	Grade-level-range
1	Number Concepts	NC	1.0–7.9
2	Horizontal Addition	HA	1.0–4.4
3	Horizontal Subtraction	HS	1.6–4.4
4	Vertical Addition	VA	1.5–5.8
5	Vertical Subtraction	VS	1.6–4.4
6	Equations	EQ	2.0–7.9
7	Measurement	MS	2.0–7.8
8	Horizontal Multiplication	HM	2.6–5.8
9	Laws of Arithmetic	LW	3.0–6.8
10	Vertical Multiplication	VM	3.5–7.8
11	Division	DV	3.5–7.8
12	Fractions	FR	4.0–7.9
13	Decimals	DC	4.0–7.9
14	Negative Numbers	NG	6.0–7.9

tions, applications, metric measurement, multiplication, problem solving, division, fractions, and decimals. The strands now mix horizontal and vertical exercises in addition, subtraction, and multiplication. Problem solving was added to the curriculum. Additional enrichment packages provide strands in geometry as well.

A student's initial grade placement is ascertained during his first ten sessions. The adjustment by half-year positions (such as 1.0, 1.5, 2.0, etc.) is based on the following scores during the first ten sessions. 50% or less correct moves a student down to the next lowest half-year level; a score of 95% or more moves a student up to the next highest half-year level.

A student session normally consists of a mixture of exercises from different strands. Exercises in a particular strand are chosen from three eqivalence classes—the one the student is in, the one below, and the one above. The mixture is determined and weighted according to the emphasis placed on the different strands within the standard elementary curriculum. For example, in grade 4 students encounter every strand but negative numbers. In a typical session a student is given about twenty exercises from different strands. The session lasts for about five to ten minutes. Table 2.2 shows the average percentage of exercises presented to a student from each strand per half year (Suppes, Searle, Kanz, and Martin Clinton 1972 (revised 1977), p. 7).

Table 2.2
Curriculum distribution. Percentage of exercises for each strand for each half year

		1.0	1.5	2.0	2.5	3.0	3.5	4.0	4.5	5.0	5.5	6.0	6.5	7.0	7.5
							HALF-GRADE LEVEL								
STRAND	NC	50	30	20	15	10	5	8	10	10	15	10	10	14	14
	HA	50	30	25	20	15	10	5	1	1					
	HS		15	15	12	10	5	2	1	1					
	VA		15	15	15	15	10	6	2	2	2	1	1		
	VS		10	10	15	15	10	10	5	2	2	1	1		
	EQ			10	10	20	20	18	15	10	12	12	10	15	15
	MS					5	5	5	8	8	8	8	5	4	4
	HM				8	5	10	8	8	10	5	1	1		
	LW				5	5	5	5	5	6	6	2	2	1	1
	VM						10	10	15	10	5	5	5	7	7
	DV						10	13	15	15	10	10	10	14	14
	FR							5	10	15	20	25	20	15	15
	DC							5	5	10	15	20	25	20	20
	NG											5	10	10	10

Reprinted with permission.

In a typical interaction with the computer the student is presented with an exercise, say

9 * 5 = __ .

The computer reacts to the student's response in the following ways. If the student types the correct answer then a new exercise is presented. If the student types the wrong answer or waits too long before replying (anywhere from ten to forty seconds is the delay time), the computer responds

TRY AGAIN,

and re-presents the exercise:

9 * 5 = __ .

If the student again makes an error, the computer types out the correct answer

9 * 5 = 45,

and then

TRY AGAIN,

and re-presents the problem yet another time:

9 * 5 = __ .

If the student again makes an error, the computer types the correct answer and then goes on to the next exercise. The exercise in which the error occurred will be presented to the student at a later time. This example follows the stimulus reinforcement strategy. The student is marked wrong for any error, but the computer gives the student three opportunities to learn the answer.

Stanford CAI and CCC

Computer Curriculum Corporation (CCC) founded in 1967 by Suppes and two associates, offers "drill and practice" in different basic subject areas: mathematics, reading, and language arts. The mathematics materials range from the first-grade level through the elementary years and into high school. The other materials begin at the third-grade level. These materials are based on research conducted at Stanford University, where a laboratory for investigating learning and teaching was set up at the IMSSS under the direction of Patrick Suppes, Richard Atkinson, and William Estes; the research commenced in 1963, when a Digital Equipment Corporation PDP-1 computer arrived.[1] For the next four years a large research effort was directed toward developing supplementary materials for elementary mathematics. (Under Atkinson's direction an elementary reading project was pursued.)

The development of the courseware for this project is linked to the development of the computer hardware and software. Using computers as teachers became a practical (economical) idea when time-sharing of the computer environment became a reality in the early 1960s. The first computer-assisted instructional program available at the Stanford laboratory was in elementary logic and was used experimentally with a few sixth graders in December 1963.[2]

Development and experimentation with arithmetic programs for first graders as well as for fourth graders were carried on from 1964 to 1965. This early first-grade arithmetic program used graphics (picture) facilities. This presentation of material did not become part of the drill-and-practice programs of CCC because of the prohibitive cost of the graphics. The logic instructional programs also did not become part of the programs, again for economic reasons: the logic programs required a large amount of computer work space, whereas the arithmetic drill programs designed for the fourth graders could operate in a small work space. Thus the arithmetic project without graphics has become the substance of the CCC mathematics curriculum. Recently, a computer system has been made available to support the logic programs, and the logic course is now available.

The reading materials initially prepared for first graders used computer-controlled audio as well as graphics facilities. Because these hardware components were costly, the CCC reading and language arts materials began with third graders, until recently. Now that CCC offers a digital speech system, the reading program starts in the first grade.

Work in logic has continued to be a major activity in Suppes's laboratory, but the level has shifted from elementary school to college, where larger expenditures on computational resources are acceptable. At Stanford University courses in logic and axiomatic set theory became routinely offered through the computer. Current research in Suppes's lab is giving considerable attention to developing more intelligent logic teaching programs.

The PDP-1 in 1963 had 32K (K=1024) words of memory, 18-bit word size, and additional storage in disks—a small machine by today's standards, and yet its memory and power were shared among several users. In those days the availability of computing power on an individual, interactive basis was such an enormous improvement over batch processing and punched cards and long turnaround time for feedback that compromises encountered by the tightness of the individual's workspace was something that could be coded around. The arithmetic project initially dealt with the compactness of work space by running only one concept block at any one time. More advanced programming techniques were developed along with the extension of the computer's memory.

Suppes separated instructional procedures—the drill-driver routines—from lesson material. The lesson material was prepared by a team of curriculum developers and entered into the computer by a team of coders. A team of programmers developed programs in machine language to control and monitor the student's performance. Thus, in the first round of implementation the materials were completely scripted, hand coded; the entire exercise and the answers were stored in the computer. This implementation was either a result of naivete about what computers are good for or a clearcut translation of behaviorist theory into practice where the world, its stimuli and responses are completely defined. Now the computer generates the numerical values in the exercises and computes the answers (Suppes, Jerman, and Brian 1968, p. 6) and the exercises are no longer stored in the computer.

The CCC materials were adapted to Hewlett-Packard, IBM, and RCA computer equipment, to name just a few. Eventually, CCC settled on designing turnkey systems, dedicated to the presentation of their materials.[3]

Attractive Features

Perhaps the most unusual characteristic of this system is that it seems to make good on its promises. For the most part, CCC materials are being used to help students who are categorized as academically and economically disadvantaged. They are for the most part low income and minority students. (Special funding from government programs have been available to purchase CCC materials.) By using CCC materials these students' scores on standardized tests improve. In contrast to what happens to similar students who do not use the CCC materials, this computer system has become attractive for many school systems.

The CCC elementary mathematics curriculum has a long history of development. The first materials were put on a computer in 1964 for first and fourth graders. By 1967 the program included materials for grades 1 through 6, and more than 1500 students were involved; and from 1967 to 1968 "approximately 1000 students in California, 600 students in Mississippi, 1100 students in Kentucky" were involved (Suppes and Morningstar 1969, p. 343). These materials have continued to reach a large number of students as school systems have leased or purchased computer systems from CCC. These materials have also been widely copied and imitated. (There has even been litigation over copyright issues.)

The CCC materials show statistically significant improvement in test scores of "economically disadvantaged" students. Typically, middle class students do not show as much improvement after this treatment. By 1969 the success of these materials was clearest with students who began from an academic position below their grade level; for example, fourth graders at third-grade level would end up at fourth-grade level after a CCC experience. (But most of them would still be below grade level as entering fifth graders.)

Suppes's approach is attractive to different people for different reasons. "Theorists" like it because it has a clear intellectual structure and scientific pedigree. "Hard-nosed empiricists" like it because its effects can be measured. "Administrators" like it because its cost structure is clear. "Teachers" like it because they are free to do other activities.

Intellectual Background

Suppes comes from two relevant traditions. He is a Stanford professor with faculty appointments in philosophy and in psychology. As a logician he sees mathematics as made up of discrete formulas or propositions; as a behaviorist, he sees behavior as made up of discrete stimulus-response units. The two obviously fit and work together in the development of this learning environment.

Suppes's active involvement in children's learning of mathematics began in the mid-1950s in a precomputer setting. He coauthored two textbooks "for primary-grade students in geometry" (Suppes 1978, p. 268). He also began to study mathematical concept formation in children, applying "as directly and naturally as possible stimulus-sampling theory to the learning of such concepts."

We met with more success than I initially expected. The ability of relatively simple models of stimulus-sampling theory to account for the learning of simple mathematical concepts in great detail, is, I think, a surprising and an important one. (Suppes 1978, p. 269).

This research on concept formation provided a foundation for Suppes's elementary school mathematics textbook series, *Sets and Numbers*, published in the 1960s, and, of course, also provided a theoretical base for his CAI work.

From a research standpoint, one of my own strong motivations for becoming involved in computer-assisted instruction was the opportunity it presented of studying subject-matter learning in the schools under conditions approximating those we ordinarily expect in a psychological laboratory. (Suppes 1978, p. 272)

Thus CAI enabled Suppes to collect a large amount of data on elementary school mathematics, which he and his co-workers have written about in numerous publications over the years. The reading group under Atkinson has also written about their findings.

Suppes has become more deeply involved in CAI at the college level and sees that "even a subject as relatively simple as elementary-school mathematics is of unbounded complexity in terms of understanding the underlying psychological theory of learning and performance" (Suppes 1978, p. 272). And like other psychologists, Suppes has looked to the ideas embedded in computing to offer alternative approaches to dealing with complex behavior. "The new ideas are more cognitive in character and organized around the concept of procedures or programs" (Suppes 1978, p. 272), which for Suppes is exemplified by "a simple register machine, that is, a simple idealized computer with a certain number of registers and a small, fixed number of instructions" (Suppes 1978, p. 272). This conceptualization fits within a behaviorist model, in which knowledge is composed of local facts, the environment (stimuli) is controlled and the internal organization is well defined. Whether this information-processing model resolves the "big" questions that Suppes would like to answer—such as what the underlying theories of learning and performance are—is part of the future.

The new approach indicates that the model of learning underlying the CCC elementary school mathematics is not sufficient to handle the complexities encountered in teaching logic, for example. In talking about his work in college level CAI Logic courses, Suppes says he is "struggling to understand how to analyze data from the sorts of proofs or logical derivations students give in the first order logic course or in the course on axiomatic set theory that follows it" (Suppes 1978, p. 272). These "skills of logical inference" involve complex student behavior for which the psychological model Suppes used in other areas does not offer enough conceptual tools for the more complex task. The new shift to computers as models for thinking is, nonetheless, viewed through the eyes of a behaviorist. It contrasts with the other views, as envisioned by each of the other proponents, discussed in this book.

Evaluation

This learning environment is easy to evaluate. It is built on a statistical model and thus lends itself to evaluations. The evaluative studies carried on by Suppes and his co-workers in his laboratory and at CCC show that students who use the system improve as indicated by their test score in the subject area. These improvements are modest, but the improvements occur in low income, economically impacted schools in which the students normally do not show improvement on standardized tests, such as the Stanford Achievement Test or the Comprehensive Test of Basic Skills.

Within the framework of drill and practice there has been a shift in emphasis as to what parameters have predictive value on student's performance. Initially the response time of the students received attention in the predictive models. Although time is still a factor, attention is now on the total time spent using the learning environment rather than latency factors in individual responses. The issue is not so much on predicting behavior on the next exercise as on predicting grade level (achievement) after a number of sessions. This predictive model is being applied to the elementary school curricula and to college courses (Larsen et al. 1978; Macken and Suppes 1976; Macken et al. 1976).

Although Suppes finds a linear relationship between amount of time spent using CAI and grade placement, he "would not expect to be able to find linear gains with indefinite increases in the amount of time spent at computer terminals" (Macken and Suppes 1976, p. 34). One CCC report strongly recommends a schedule of ten minutes per day per curriculum—resulting in 1500 minutes of CAI time per year per curriculum—in order to achieve maximum effectiveness (Poulsen and Macken 1978, p. 1). According to this report evaluators often choose the mean gain as a criterion of success: "Mean gains [should increase at least one month for each month of instruction. Such a growth pattern would be a significant improvement for typical CAI students whose growth rate prior to CAI is not more than .7 months per month'' (Poulsen and Macken 1978, p. 3).

The CCC curriculum has its clearest success with students who perform below their grade level according to their scores on standardized tests. Whether these students are at schools for the deaf, Indian schools, or in Freeport, New York, or Los Nietos, California, their standardized test scores typically improve during the years they use the CCC systems. Evaluative studies conducted between 1971 and 1977 indicate a pattern in which the students show a grade placement improvement of 1 to 1.5 years at the end of their experience in mathematics and about 0.6 year in reading or language arts. From 1976 to 1980, a study on the effects of the CCC materials on students in the Los Angeles Unified School District was conducted by Educational Testing Service. In 1982, an Educational Testing Service evaluation of the CCC material in the Los Angeles Unified School District was published. The study found that students made significant gains on their computational skills. The reading and language arts materials did not reflect the same kind of increased improvement in test scores. The test scores did increase in the first year, but in additional years there was no increase (and no decrease) in test scores (Ragosta 1983, 1979; Ragosta et al. 1982).

CCC introduced materials developed in the Stanford Laboratory into schools. This transfer has been conducted with considerable support and care to preserve the laboratory conditions. CCC sells a complete system with clusters of terminals. The number of computers in a configuration can be as small as four. Typically, the system is purchased with funds allocated for poor, minority populations (Title 1, for example). A configuration of sixteen to thirty-two terminals is normally put in a separate room and staffed by someone trained to use the material and aid trainees. Suppes, the originator of the delivery system, has full control over the dispersal of his ideas.

Suppes has developed a CAI logic course for Stanford undergraduates. He has worked with other Stanford faculty to develop courses to teach languages, such as Russian. The strategy is the same. The material is broken down into small components, and the learner is led through a sequence, which has a few possible branches depending on the user's responses. These courses have been used by Stanford students. The amount of critical knowledge that has gone into the development of these courses is considerable. The programming has been demanding, and the content has been developed over several years of debugging.

For many educators the tests and the style of delivery raise questions as to what children are learning about mathematics. They often argue about whether to use Suppes's materials. Those who think that the content and delivery developed by Suppes is what children should be learning will want to use his materials, as they are probably the most thoroughly debugged. Another question is whether drill and practice is by itself an appropriate means of communicating a taste for mathematics learning. I do not think anyone would doubt that practice is a necessary ingredient in learning. The problem of keeping practice from turning into mindless drill is linked to teaching strategies and the learner's control over his own learning.

The model of a student using the elementary math material is simple. Davis builds a more complex picture of a student learning mathematics, as we will see in the next chapter. The range and kinds of activities is wider. For Suppes this is irrelevant. For Davis the style of interaction is important to reassure children's intellectual curiosity.

Some Criticisms

Suppes claims that the CCC materials are representative of the current curricula in schools and offers to provide students with a way to meet minimal competency requirements in "basic skills." Sections of the Stanford Achievement Test do bear a striking resemblance to the exercise presentation of the CCC math strands. Thus there is strong support for his materials within the traditional folds of education. There are others in mathematics education who view an elementary mathematics education that is quite different from the one espoused by Suppes. Nonetheless, Suppes's reductionist approach to elementary mathematics reopens the debate as to what minimal skills children must acquire and what other mathematical activities should take place in the classroom outside of the CAI environment. Is this CAI environment conveying a sense of real mathematics through its drill-and-practice exercises? Suppes often suggests that his materials are meant to supplement regular classroom activities. But what if there are no other activities? Will these activities provide children with the real basic skills that will enable them to become mathematically minded, to be good problem solvers in everyday life?

An essential weakness and paradox of the CCC learning environment is that it is based on a psychological theory that is statistically satisfying but of extremely limited scope. As Suppes himself points out, this simple learning model does not account for complexities encountered in other areas of mathematics learning, such as in logic. In a sense, then, this theory is *ad hoc*, and although research supporting it occupies a major activity for psychologists and educational researchers, the nature of the domain remains *ad hoc*.

There are some interesting consequences to this turning of psychological theory into educational foundations. For example, response time, a key parameter of so many activities in learning experiments, becomes a relatively minor factor—it remains part of the reinforcement strategy but has less predictive value over long-term performance in the learning environment. Because the learning enviroment does not achieve impressive results with middle class student populations in suburban settings (Suppes and Morningstar 1969) this whole system dramatically implies a picture of schooling that is "out of sync" with its students.

The argument so often perpetuated for justifying the elementary math curriculum as it is or as "basic skills" programs present it is that people need those skills. As we will see in the following chapters of this book, what these basic skills are is part of an ongoing controversy and it is not just a matter of old math versus new math.

CCC for the 1980s

In the 1980s, the focus of the use of computers in schools is on small personal computers rather than on time-shared computers. The computer-as-textbook, as implemented by Suppes, requires a large central storage area that can be accessed by individual terminals. Suppes offers a dedicated time-shared environment that runs the CCC materials exclusively. These CAI systems need memory not only to run and store the programs and their canned responses but also to keep track of the student's performance and attendance. Large urban school systems, such as Los Angeles, Chicago, and Philadelphia, with large populations of students who could benefit from remedial programs, continue to be heavy users of Suppes's systems.

CCC has been improving and expanding the capabilities of its systems. The number and range of materials have grown as the hardware has changed. For example, in 1980 CCC introduced a digital speech system, which can store up to 1000 minutes of speech sounds. The prerecorded messages can be complete sentences, phrases, and words. This audio system has been used in a couple of ways. In the Chicago area, for instance, students participate in Dial-a-Drill. Using a touchtone telephone at home, either the student phones the computer or the computer phones the student, and for six minutes a day the computer speaks to the student, giving the student math problems. The student responds by pressing the touchtone telephone keys. This mental arithmetic activity had been investigated in Suppes's Stanford lab many years before. Now it is commercially available.

The digital audio system allowed the enhancement of another area of instruction—teaching English as a second language. Courses are available for native speakers of Spanish, Japanese, and Chinese. The digital audio / speech system contains, besides many words, phrases, and sentences, some intonation rules and rules of grammar. Thus it can generate unanticipated sentences from its collection of words. For the most part, however, the lessons select stored sentences and phrases. There are over 600 hours of instructional materials and thus many hours of recorded speech.

With the audio system in operation, the early reading program for first and second graders is now available. The reading program also includes a second-grade reading course that does not use the audio system.

In the spring of 1984, CCC introduced its own computer system based on a 68000 processor using the UNIX operating system. The terminals used in this system support minimal graphics. Thus the elementary mathematics materials now use bar graphs and line graphs. Other changes in the strands have been made to include positive and negative numbers in upper elementary school. The fractions strand has been revised to present the material in vertical form (that is, $\frac{1}{2}$) rather than in horizontal form (that is, $1/2$). A new strand, called problem-solving, has been added to the math curriculum; it starts in the third grade. Another change in the way the elementary mathematics curriculum operates is a feature called selected drill. It has to do with the teacher's role. The teacher can enact selected skills. If some part of the CCC curriculum is not relevant to the teacher's curriculum, it can be avoided.

The range of courses also includes the teaching of programming languages such as BASIC and Pascal; a computer literacy course, in which a subset of BASIC is taught; a turtle graphics experience (text oriented); and a simple register machine environment. A logic course for junior high school students is also available. A mail facility, allowing users to send messages to one another, is now beginning to work as well. In the future a writing skills course will be offered; it will be linked to a word processing system developed by the CCC staff. The word processor will be menu driven, not unlike the Bank Street Writer, but it will be expandable to a more advanced word processor. The system will also support remote clusters of eight or sixteen terminals.

The Microhost System

The Microhost computer configuration is designed for expandability. At this point one processor is used alone, but CCC intends to allow up to three 68000s to run together. A single 68000 system can have one, two, or four megabytes of memory and either one or two 40-megabyte hard disks. A system consisting of one megabyte of memory and one disk drive can support forty terminals running the math and reading strands. If the language arts strand were also in use, then the system would support thirty-two terminals.

The costs for such a system would probably be in the neighborhood of $70,000 to $100,000. The computer would cost about $20,000. The terminals are about $1000 each. Then on top of that there are maintenance fees for courses, software licensing fees, and so on. Subscribers can change their course selection. If audio/speech capabilities are wanted, there is an additional charge of up to $1000 per terminal.

Materials

The materials continue to be evaluated not only by the company but also by the school systems. Although the subject matter varies, the style of interaction does not. The student is guided along a carefully analyzed path. The emphasis within each subject area is on formal manipulations.

Most of the course materials offered by CCC were derived from research paths pursued under Suppes's direction at Stanford. As computers have become cheaper and more powerful, he has been able to replicate the research and turn it into viable commercial products.

CAI on Microcomputers

Materials in the style of CCC's have been developed for microcomputers and offered commercially. But there are differences between the systems on microcomputers today and the CCC time-shared systems. There are differences in the quality of the material, in the degree to which the materials have been debugged, and in the smoothness of the delivery. Perhaps the most significant difference lies in the delivery—what the students and teachers must do and what the computer automatically does. The programs themselves are not complicated and are not very big. (Actually, generating drill-and-practice arithmetic materials are popular programming projects for children.) The algorithms for selecting material become more complicated. Keeping a permanent record of each student's progress adds another complication and requires permanent storage. Moreover, additional programs are needed to print reports. CAI in other subject areas such as reading, require considerable permanent storage to contain all the material. The differences between a time-shared computing environment, whose only task is to run CCC materials, and the typical school microcomputer setup show up in the way that the functions of presenting material and keeping track of student performance are integrated.

In some school settings, clusters of microcomputers are loosely linked together by sharing one large permanent storage device. Often, the microcomputers have individual floppy disk drives for saving a student's work or for accessing programs not on the permanent storage disk. In other school settings, the microcomputers stand alone. A student in these typical settings might have to learn things about using the computer that have nothing to do with the CAI session. In fact, the student's ten minute session might have to be stretched to much longer sessions to take into account loading and saving of files from floppy diskettes.

In contrast, CCC students are hardly aware of the computer as distinct from the drill-and-practice presentation. Students are not aware of floppy diskettes or other hardware parts. They sit down at a terminal and log in (identify themselves to the computer). The computer then presents a set of materials to them based on the recorded past history of the students' performances. Periodically, a summary of this history is given to the student. At the end of the day (week, month) the computer operator prints out reports on each of the students for their teachers. Thus records and course materials sequenced differently for each student are automatically and almost invisibly provided to the users. CCC also offers a large selection of courses. Typical microcomputer setups might offer a range of materials, but students have to be aware of the computer and its operating system.

As more powerful microcomputers come into fashion in schools, the ease with which CAI materials can be delivered will increase. Stand-alone machines, that is, individual workstations, are compelling. For example, CCC adapted some of its materials to run on a Sony (SMC-70) microcomputer. The computer and the delivery of the courseware have had limited appeal. More powerful microcomputers were needed. CCC has renewed its attempt at packaging a stand-alone system and has chosen the Atari 520 ST. It can act as a terminal to the Microhost system, but will be available as a self-contained CCC Learning Station. Priced at about $2000 or $3000 and equipped with two floppy disks and a hard disk drive, it will come with Atari's word processor, Logo, and BASIC, and CCC courseware. The Microhost system might remain the system of choice. On the other hand, the Atari 520 ST might greatly increase the community of users, which is said to be on the order of 500,000 (Mace 1985). Perhaps future evaluations will hinge on differences in the delivery of CCC materials in a dedicated time-shared environment of the Microhost and the materials delivered in the context of a stand-alone station.

3

Davis: Socratic Interactions and Discovery Learning

Davis's vision of what elementary mathematics is and how it should be taught contrasts sharply with Suppes's views. For Davis, mathematics is part of the real everyday life experiences of children. It is essential to the development of the curriculum that mathematics draw on this reality and bring the children's experiences into the mathematics classroom. As a developmentalist, Davis observed children's activities and concluded that children bring to school active minds rich with many years of experience. A good curriculum should not create a gap between school activities and non-school experiences. Rather it should build on both experiences because they interrelate. Davis does not see mathematics as a hierarchy of discrete number facts or a sequence of logical statements. For him, mathematics includes arithmetic but consists of many other areas some of which rely on arithmetic foundations and help children deal with real world phenomena.

Davis sees mathematics as a creative activity and is eager to show children that there are different ways to do things and that they themselves can invent unique ways. One of Davis's favorite examples of children's discovery in the mathematics classroom is Kye, a third grader who invented his own algorithm for subtraction. When encouraged by his teacher, Kye felt confident enough in what he had achieved to stand by his method. The story points to a relationship between the creativity of children and the sensitivity of teachers.

Kye's Story

... in Weston, Connecticut, a third grade teacher was discussing the subtraction problem

$$\begin{array}{r} 64 \\ -28 \\ \hline \end{array}$$

and was saying something of the familiar sort "I can't take 8 from 4, so I regroup the 64 as 50 plus 14" (or whatever), when a third grade boy named Kye interrupted:

"Oh, yes, you can. Four minus eight is negative four ...

```
  64
 -28
 ----
  -4
```

and twenty from sixty is forty

```
  64
 -28
 ----
  -4
  40
```

and forty and negative four is thirty-six

```
  64
 -28
 ----
  -4
 -40
 ----
 -36."
```

(Davis 1965, pp. 3–4)

Davis applies mathematical knowledge to mathematics itself; he sees classical mathematics as a rich and growing body of ideas. It is open-ended and expandable and should be taught that way. There are many unsolved as well as undiscovered problems in mathematics. Davis believes that children can contribute to this growing body of mathematical knowledge. Of course, there are some strategies and techniques that Davis sees as foundational to doing creative mathematics.

Discovery Learning and Teaching Strategies

The vision of elementary school mathematics education as embodied in the University of Illinois Plato computer system is based on the Madison Project, a research and development effort started by Davis in 1957. This project is named for the Madison School in Syracuse, New York. The Madison Project method makes extensive use of what Davis calls the "paradigm teaching strategy," in which new ideas are introduced through carefully chosen examples (Davis et al. 1978, p. 273). In this situation a teacher concretely builds on what a child already knows. For example, in introducing children to fractions they are first asked to share a candy bar with three friends. Then they are told that each piece is one-third of the candy bar. Children know how to share a candy bar; they have done it often. Thus the teacher relates the mathematics to what the child already knows, and the image remains sharp for the child.

Another teaching strategy that Davis employs is presenting a child with a challenge. In a sense, this is the opposite of the paradigm teaching strategy.

Ask the child to do something he or she has never done before, then give the child help in the form of examples, hints, etc. For example, a rather well-known Madison Project activity is the "Guess My Rule" game. The child suggests a number, to which the teacher responds with another number computed from a rule, such as $x + 3 = y$ (the child's number being x and the teacher's being y). The game continues with the child trying to formulate the relationship or "rule" formally as an equation.

There are other examples of this teaching strategy throughout the Plato math. The strategy builds on the observation that children are challenged by their environments everyday; thus they should be challenged in the math classroom, where eventually a rational explanation will be forthcoming. The process can serve as an example of how it is possible to meet challenges and sometimes to solve the problem without "help." Often as the problem is resolved, the child sees that this new knowledge is developed out of what is already known. Perhaps one important aspect of this is that the challenges interest the children and are based on Davis's knowledge about children and mathematics. He has a definite content in mind and a view of activities that children like to do within that content area. Plato allows us to see this content—to see children interacting with these teaching strategies and to see where conflicts and misunderstandings between what the teacher (Plato) expects and what the child does occur. We can see weaknesses in the presentation. We can also see the strengths of visual, interactive, dynamic, and changing imagery in the presentation. The textbook becomes alive. The curriculum with its features and drawbacks becomes one for "my children if only..." rather than "good for other people's children."

The Madison Project and Teachers

The Madison Project attempted to encourage children's mathematical development through "discovery" and so built up a repertoire of paradigm teaching strategies. The following statement summarizes this view of mathematics. For Davis

mathematics is complex and creative; subtle aspects are important; actual thought processes are important, and differ from one child to another (although there *are* important underlying patterns); "discovery learning," under appropriate conditions, is highly desirable; an elaborate pattern of ideas must be built up in a child's head, and only the child can build it; it is the teacher's job to help the child to build up this elaborate structure of interrelated ideas, and to help the child correct the structure of interrelated ideas, and to help the child correct the structure whenever it is found to be in error. (Davis 1979, p. 77)

We will find Dwyer saying similar things. The question is, How is this possible for teachers?

For Davis teachers can be compared with actors who function in two different capacities: by "presenting well-rehearsed lines scripted by someone else" and by improvising or "responding in a new and unique way to a new and unique challenge" (Davis 1979, p. 58). Thus the Madison Project activites were "carefully crafted and carefully tested" and "intended to be taught with careful fidelity to the 'script'" and so teachers were given extensive training toward this end. At the same time they were given experiences to encourage their own spontaneous behavior (Davis 1979, p. 58). To accomplish this the Madison Project used the following methods (Davis 1979, p. 60):

a) In trial teaching, carefully "scripted" units were developed, refined and tested.

b) Procedures for handling the "flexible" or "spontaneous" or "responsive" part of teaching were worked out, again using direct trials with students *as part of the design process itself* (and NOT merely for testing *after* design work was done).

c) Typical classroom lessons were recorded on film or videotape, so that other teachers could see for themselves *exactly what* was done, and exactly *what the resulting outcome was.*

d) A large teacher education program was set up, in cooperation with the public school systems in Chicago, San Diego County, New York City, Los Angeles, Philadelphia, and elsewhere, that reached over 30,000 teachers.

These materials were created through direct observation of classroom activity, descriptions of actual interactions with individual children and analysis of the mathematics being taught. Thus Davis developed his math materials from his own classroom teaching and from the work of other people teaching and reporting on their experiences.

Thus the Madison Project had several components, among them developing concepts and making materials. Along these lines its plans were easily fulfilled. But one central component of its activities was much more difficult: the new vision of mathematics would work only if it was adopted by teachers. And the adoption had to be more than intellectual and verbal; it had to be translated into behavior, it had to be accepted in the gut as well as in the head. It was here that the Madison Project ran into obstacles. But the teachers could be trained to use the materials and follow the "script," and thousands did through summer workshops.

The following anecdote captures the root of the problem. A teacher who had taken part in a workshop on "discovery learning" came back almost in tears complaining that the students had "discovered it wrong." Bob Davis himself and his virtuoso disciples could work with a class of children, sensitively guiding the discovery process. In particular, they could pick out the germs of good insight in what the less understanding teacher saw as simply "wrong." The problem is deep: People brought up with a view of mathematics as discrete facts to be mastered do not easily discard this view. The reformer is faced with the problem:

We cannot tell teachers all they need to know about teaching—we must choose. Indeed, we must choose not merely content, but also the *kind* of content, and in fact even the media by which and form in which this "knowledge" is presented. (Davis 1967, p. 60)

The problem is compounded by what happens in the next year with "untrained" teachers.

I believe that Plato represents for Davis a possible way out of the trap. Perhaps the computer can be programmed to do at least part of what the teachers could not learn. Perhaps some characteristics of the best teachers can be embodied in well-constructed programs. Of course, not everything can be translated into programs and Davis does not want the Plato mathematics units to replace human teachers. But some aspects of a good teacher's strategies could be captured in a machine.

Contrasting Suppes and Davis

Before describing in more detail the Plato elementary mathematics curriculum, its features, and its weaknesses, it might be helpful to first contrast Suppes, the behaviorist, and Davis, the developmentalist.

Both Suppes and Davis were curriculum reformers before Sputnik. After Sputnik there was considerable curriculum reform in response to popular feelings that society's needs for mathematicians and scientists were not being met. Suppes and Davis go in different directions in their visions of mathematics, their theories of learning and their underlying philosophy of education. They both saw the need for change but in different ways.

Suppes's first involvement in elementary mathematics was motivated by his daughter entering school in the mid-1950s. His dissatisfaction with her introduction to mathematics inspired him to coauthor a geometry book for the primary grades (Suppes 1978). Davis, on the other hand, became an elementary education reformer by intent, not by accident. As a mathematician and teacher of mathematics at the university level, he reasoned that, if you want to develop mathematicians, then you must create conditions for children to "develop" into mathematicians. If you want to create thinkers, then you must create conditions that do not repress children's thinking. In visiting classrooms in the mid-1950s, Davis was shocked and chagrined by what he saw. In the first place, the content was far removed from anything that would give children a sense of being mathematicians. They were taught the laws of arithmetic without any content or context in which to use them, with the exception of business applications (percent problems, bank balances, etc.). Davis saw the need to broaden the curriculum. He wanted to include the study of algebra, coordinate geometry, logical implication, graphing, and functions as areas of mathematics in which arithmetic could be applied.

Davis saw that reforms were needed that went beyond the curriculum itself, encompassing the classroom environment and the ways teachers relate to students. He reacted strongly against the dominant educational theory in the pre-Sputnik period. Often, he vitriolically castigated the behaviorist approach to learning based on a model of the child as an empty vessel into which knowledge, organized as discrete bits of information, is poured by the teacher. He is fond of saying: The purpose of that kind of mathematics teaching is to make the child say the right answer no matter what he believes.

Davis wanted to broaden the content of elementary mathematics. He wanted to teach children mathematics in a style that emulates a mathematician's exiences. He wanted to create a curriculum that would build on children's natural curiosity and allow them to ''discover'' the laws of mathematics for themselves. Doing this would require changes in the curriculum. It would require teachers to develop a ''discovery'' style of teaching, and it would require a classroom environment that would contribute to this process.

Suppes's reformist period involved him in proposing changes to the mathematics curriculum by introducing set theory as the foundation for mathematical knowledge. (Geometry, logic, and other direct applications of set theoretic ideas were major content thrusts that Suppes attempted to introduce into the primary grades.) The path to this reform was through writing better textbooks for teachers and children, not in changing the traditional style of teaching; Suppes believed that, if the ''right knowledge'' were properly organized, then schools would produce citizens to meet society's needs. Suppes gave up his ''reformist'' activities and has become a symbol of ''arch conservatism.'' In part, his system is a castigation of the training and preparation of teachers as it attempts to replace them in their role of teacher (not in their role of custodian) while supporting the traditions of the preformist period of drill and practice in arithmetic.

Davis continues to pursue his reformist goals and has remained an outspoken critic of Suppes, rote learning, set theory in elementary school, and the narrowness of the pre-Sputnik mathematics curriculum, with its concentration on and failure at developing ''basic mathematics skills.'' After many years of curriculum development, teacher workshops, and demonstration classes, Davis began to explore the possibility of the computer as a discovery learning environment.

Details of Some Plato Materials

Plato is a time-shared computer designed to be used by hundreds of people at the same time. Students access the Plato computer system through graphics terminals. The quality of the plasma panel technology supported both pictures and text displayed on the screen. The elementary math materials make heavy use of this picture-making facility. The computer becomes an interactive textbook with graphics illustrations, which can be changed by the children's actions.

Sharing Jumping Beans: Paradigm Teaching Strategy
This lesson is one of several exemplifying Davis's paradigm teaching strategy. Instead of breaking up candy bars, for example, children are asked to share a box of jumping beans among the figures appearing on the Plato screen (figure 3.1). The number of figures can vary from two to five. Children interact with the lesson by touching the graphics screen in different locations.

West: Challenge
West captures the excitement and challenge of Madison Project's "Guess My Rule" games. One of the most appealing of the Plato lessons, West (figure 3.2) is based on the classical children's board game *Chutes and Ladders*. Children make their plays by forming mathematical sentences out of three numbers randomly chosen by Plato. The playing pieces are a stagecoach and a train, which are pitted against one another in a race through eight towns with seventy-one board positions (0–70); shortcuts are randomly placed along the way. As in other board games, players can bump one another's playing pieces by landing on the same board position as that occupied by the opponent's piece. The moves are computed from three spinners displayed on the screen. The numbers on the spinners can be changed. Each spinner can be different. Negative and positive numbers are used.

The computer makes this game different from other board games in several ways, some inessential and one essential. For example, the computer moves the playing pieces to their new board positions. It causes the three spinners to "spin." It prints out these randomly selected numbers and waits for the player to form an arithmetic expression using the three numbers. Actually, the student player is expected to make up an expression,

a

Figure 3.1
Example of Share Jumping Beans. The purpose of the exercise is to define fractions (one-half, one-third, one-fourth, and one-fifth) of a set of objects. There are four problems: The student shares a box of jumping beans fairly with two to five children on the screen. © 1976, Board of Trustees, University of Illinois. Reprinted with permission.

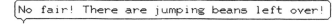

Try again!

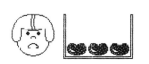

| beans |
| jump |
| ← |

beans
jump
→

b

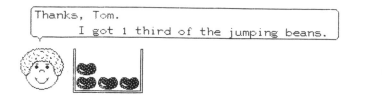

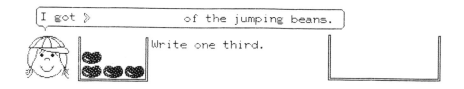

Figure 3.1c

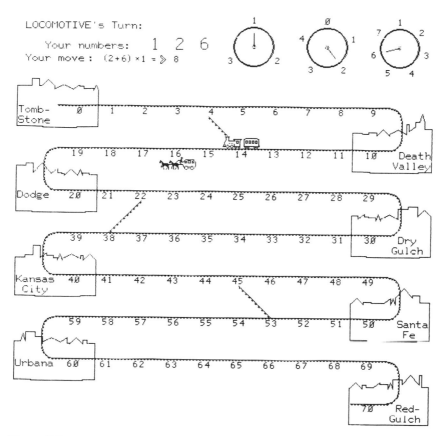

Figure 3.2

An example of the game West. The purposes of the exercise are to gain computational skills, to formulate combinations, and to develop a winning strategy. The game can be played against another student or against the computer. © 1976, Board of Trustees, University of Illinois. Reprinted with permission.

compute its result, and type the complete "sentence" into the computer. The computer then checks the expression and the result; if they are okay, the computer moves the playing piece. If the spinners, for example, point to 3, 5, and 2, the player might make one of several moves:

$$2 + 3 + 5 = 10$$
or $$3 \times 5 + 2 = 17$$
or $$3 \times (5 + 2) = 21$$
or $$3 \times 2 - 5 = 1$$
But
$$3 + 3 + 3 = 9$$
or $$3 - 2 + 5 = 4$$
or $$5 - 2 + 3 = 0$$

would not be accepted by the computer. The computer itself can be a player. In this case, Plato can set an example of how to play the game.

West captures a certain spirit of doing mathematics that is at the core of Davis's philosophy: The game attracts adult players as well as children. The way knowledge about the game spreads is by a natural word-of-mouth process. Children are not given a long list of rules to learn; instead they learn by playing the game and the game uses familiar ideas—*Chutes and Ladders*, spinners, arithmetic. The teacher is not needed to stand over the children's play but is needed as a resource to help construct "winning" expressions optimally or to make other expert moves. For timid children who do not want to "compete" against fellow students the option of playing against Plato is compelling. Thus, for some children, making a legal arithmetic expression out of the three numbers requires their full concentration. For other children developing game-playing strategies and then using the three numbers to forward their strategy becomes their focus. This is done without any explicit instruction from the computer or the teacher.

Not all the games and lessons on Plato have such a wide appeal to different age groups. The magnetism of this lesson caused it to be the focus of research on computer-based tutoring/coaching systems by John Seely Brown and colleagues at Bolt, Beranek, and Newman (Brown and Goldstein 1977; Burton and Brown 1976, 1978). West was embedded into a computer system that acted as a "coach" or advisor observing the play of the game and offering suggestions to maximize the play. Embedding West into a "coaching" environment as Brown et al. did, changes the learning environment rather dramatically from a student-directed to a "teacher-dominated" situation. The player is now being coached to choose wisely and well on each move, to make the best play, to do well, etc. The motivation for "improvement" comes now from the coach's prodding, not from the child and the activity. The coach has a certain model of what good play is and imposes this view on the player. The coach in the computer might indeed be clever and might at times have great insights into the player's strategy, but the atmosphere, the kind of learning environment has changed. West's discovery learning is transformed to a more behaviorist and teacher-controlled instruction.

Examples of Other Lessons

Unlike the CCC materials, which are divided into uniform units equivalent to tenths of grade levels, the Plato lessons vary in what they cover, the style of teaching they use, the amount of time a student is expected to spend on the lesson, the number of times the student uses the lesson, etc. A lesson can be thought of as an independent program that is linked to others in different ways. Some lessons are more encompassing than others. For example, Speedway (figure 3.3) offers drill and practice in basic arithmetic operations. It has several parts; a student chooses to enter any of four different car races. The student is presented with ten problems and given help along the way if it is needed. His or her speed is recorded and graphically compared with past performance. Each race consists of two cars, one representing the past speed and the other the current speed of the student. The speed differences are also represented on a bar graph; thus the student is exposed to different graphical representations of data.

Other lessons, such as Subtract with Sticks (figure 3.4), are more didactic in character, and are geared to show a student how to do something through a "paradigm teaching strategy"; having made the connection between bundles of sticks and place notation of numbers, followed by unbundling to show borrowing, the image can be left to the student's imagination. As the lesson progresses, the concrete visual images are suppressed. The length of time a student spends on the lesson depends on his or her performance.

Some lessons, for example, Rubber Stamp (figure 3.5), ask students to indicate their responses by touching the screen. Each time the student touches the screen within an outlined area marked "PAPER," a copy of the sample rubber stamp is made at that location. The lesson then tells the student how many stamps he or she used, asks the student to write the "addition number sentence" for that picture, and finally interprets the number sentence in words.

The Plato terminal's touch facility is used in a series of lessons in which a student represents fractions by cutting up and coloring in a fraction of a rectangle displayed on the screen. One of these "fraction" painting lessons allows the student to save his or her picture permanently in the computer

◆◆◆◆◆◆◆◆◆◆◆◆◆◆◆◆◆◆◆◆◆◆◆◆◆◆◆◆◆◆◆◆◆◆◆◆◆◆◆

What race would you like to enter?

◆◆◆◆◆◆◆◆◆◆◆◆◆◆◆◆◆◆◆◆◆◆◆◆◆◆◆◆◆◆◆◆◆◆◆◆◆◆◆

PRESS D or G or S or I:

D for DAYTONA   +   —

G for GRAND PRIX   ×

S for SEBRING   ÷

I for INDIANAPOLIS 500   +   —   ×   ÷

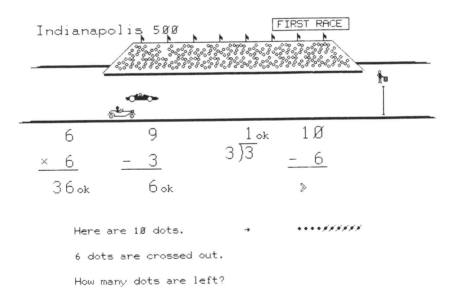

a

Figure 3.3
An example of Speedway. The purpose of the exercise is to gain speed and accuracy in solving basic addition, subtraction, multiplication, and division problems. © 1976, Board of Trustees, University of Illinois. Reprinted with permission.

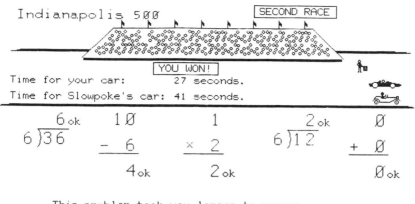

Indianapolis 5ØØ   SECOND RACE

YOU WON!

Time for your car: 27 seconds.
Time for Slowpoke's car: 41 seconds.

6 ok   1 Ø   1   2 ok   Ø
6)36   − 6   × 2   6)12   + Ø
            ‾‾‾‾   ‾‾‾‾   ‾‾‾‾
            4 ok   2 ok   Ø ok

This problem took you longer to answer.

6 ok   8   6   6 ok   1

This graph shows HOW MANY PROBLEMS YOU HAD CORRECT
for each race.

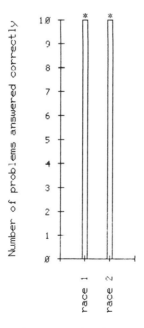

(The stars * show your best scores.)

        Press -NEXT-

b

How to borrow using sticks

▦ ▦ ▦ ▦ | | |

4 3

− 2 5

Here is a problem.
We need to take away 5 loose sticks but we only have 3.
We can get more loose sticks by opening a bundle.
Press ⌊b⌋ to open a bundle.

How to borrow using sticks

▦ ▦ ▦ | | | | | | | | | | | | |

4 3

− 2 5
‾‾‾‾‾‾‾‾

How many loose sticks are there now?

a

Figure 3.4
Two examples of Subtract with Sticks. The purpose of the exercise is to teach the subtraction algorithm. © 1976, Board of Trustees, University of Illinois. Reprinted with permission.

<u>Solve this problem.</u>

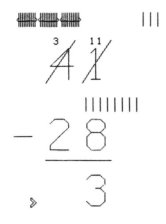

Press -LAB- if there are no tens in your answer.
Press ⎣b⎦ if you want to open a bundle.

b

48   *Chapter 3*

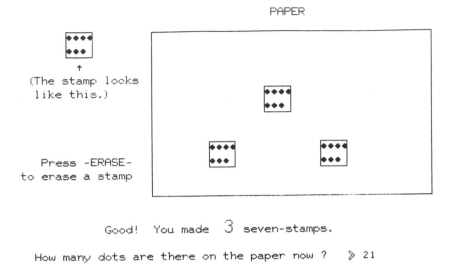

Good! You made 3 seven-stamps.

How many dots are there on the paper now ?   ⟩ 21

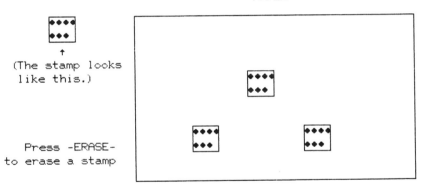

Good! You made 3 seven-stamps.

How many dots are there on the paper now ?   ⟩ 21 dots ok

Please write an addition sentence about this picture

⟩ 7 + 7 + 7 = 2 1

Good ! Press -NEXT- for a new stamp.

Figure 3.5
An example of Rubber Stamp. The purposes of the exercise are to introduce the concepts of addition and multiplication, to emphasize the correspondence between a picture and a number sentence, and to show how an addition number sentence can be interpreted in words. © 1976, Board of Trustees, University of Illinois. Reprinted with permission.

in a "library" common to other users; this additional incentive caused the students to compete with one another for original ways to represent fractions.

Many lessons use number lines to enhance their presentation. Some, such as Darts (figure 3.6) are concerned with helping students "understand the meanings of mathematical symbols. In the case of fractions, for example, it is important for the student to recognize $7/8$ or $2/35$ or 5.4 as numbers having a definite size, just as 7 or 500 do" (Davis 1977, p. 73). Other uses of number lines appear in lessons, such as Numberline Multiplication, Numberline Division, Homesweet Toadstool (another division lesson), Egg Dropper (for manipulation of signed numbers), Torpedo (fractions; figure 3.7).

Many lessons employ the strategy of Speedway (figure 3.3) in which the student competes against him- or herself, or the strategy of Painting Library (figure 3.8) in which the student competes for originality against other students. Other lessons, such as West, can be thought of as two-player games in which Plato itself could be one of the players. Other lessons that support innovative activities by the students are Spiderweb (figure 3.9) and Skywriting (figure 3.10). These lessons build on Papert's computational geometric entity, the turtle, discussed in chapter 5.

Plato Math

In describing the Plato materials, we can see that the task is different from talking about the CCC materials. The reasons for this are due to the underlying differences in Davis's and Suppes's views of content and teaching. The Plato materials use different teaching strategies and show different computational techniques for performing the basic arithmetic operations; children are asked to participate in creating exercises, which they then solve. Thus lessons differ from one another in many ways and discussions on one might not say much about another. The lessons are based on ideas developed in the Madison Project.

The Goals of the Madison Project

The aims of the Madison Project were to broaden the original content of elementary school mathematics to include not only the "algorithms of arithmetic," "fractions, ratio, percent, and applications to retail sales situations" but also "some of the fundamental concepts of algebra (such as variable, function, the arithmetic of signed numbers, open sentences, axiom, theorem, and derivations), some fundamental concepts of coordinate geometry (such as graph of a function), some ideas of logic (such as

Shoot a dart
at ⟩

a

Figure 3.6
An example of Darts. The purpose of this exercise is to estimate fractional distances
on a number line. © March 1975, Board of Trustees, University of Illinois.
Reprinted with permission.

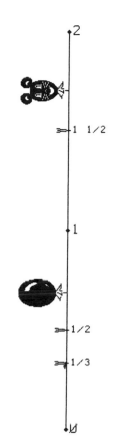

2

1 1/2

1

1/2

1/3

0

Shoot a dart
at ≫

b

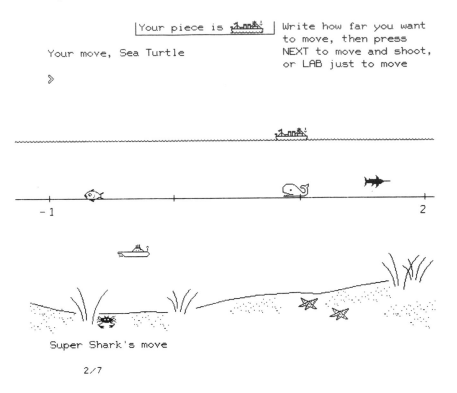

a

Figure 3.7
An example of Torpedo. The purpose of this exercise is to estimate fractional distances on a number line. © March 1975, Board of Trustees, University of Illinois. Reprinted with permission.

Your piece is 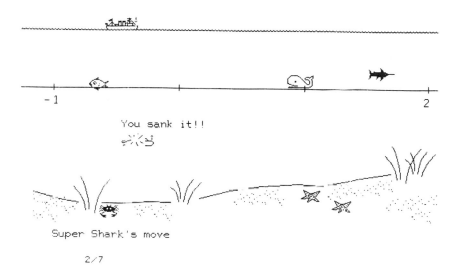 Write how far you want
to move, then press
NEXT to move and shoot,
or LAB just to move

-1.4 ok

You sank it!!

Super Shark's move

2/7

NEXT for a new game

b

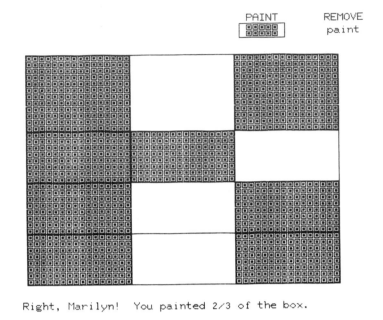

Right, Marilyn! You painted 2/3 of the box.

NEXT to try a different way   LAB to save this in the library
BACK to choose a new fraction   DATA to look at the library

a

Figure 3.8
An example of Painting Library. The purposes of the exercise are to encourage painting a fraction of the box in different ways, to initiate the idea of rearranging the painted areas without changing the fraction painted, to provide the opportunity to notice equivalent fractions, and to share the student's work with others. © March 1975, Board of Trustees, University of Illinois. Reprinted with permission.

This is how Lawston painted 5/9 of the box.

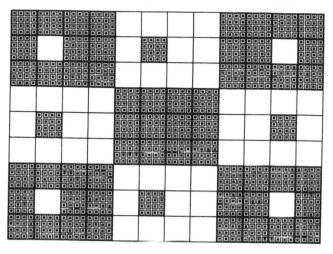

NEXT to see another painting.

BACK to the name list.
LAB to do a painting.

Paintings Library for group elrick

1.	alfred w	2/7	2/7
2.	amy b	1/4	
3.	andy h	2/7	1/4
4.	david k	1/4	
5.	edy l	1/2	
6.	james a	1/2	
7.	jeff n	6/8	5/9
8.	karen l	1/4	1/4
9.	kim g	1/2	
10.	paula g	1/4	1/2
11.	scott a	1/4	
12.	stephanie a	1/4	
13.	trent s	1/4	2/7
14.	troy r	6/8	

That's the end of this library...

Whose paintings do you want to see? ⊳
    (write the number)

To do a painting, press LAB.
To look at another library, press DATA.

b

```
  7f    1/3t      7f    1/3t      6f   1/3t      5f   1/3t      4f  r
↑                                                                  ↑
└──────────────────────────────────────────────────────────────────┘
```

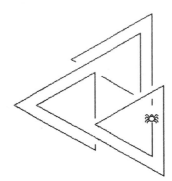

```
        stephen g -- "tri-fo"
```

a

Figure 3.9
Two examples of Spiderweb. © 1976, Board of Trustees, University of Illinois.
Reprinted with permission.

1/4t   8 f   1/4t   8 f   1/4t   8 f   1/4t   8 f 1 1/5t r

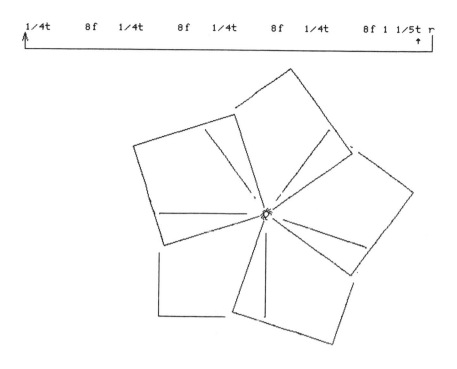

robert a -- "Square"

b

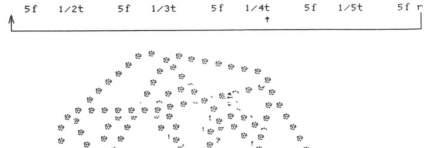

```
5f    1/2t    5f    1/3t    5f    1/4t    5f    1/5t    5f  r
```

```
linda c -- "dave'star"
```
a

Figure 3.10
Two examples of Skywriting. © 1976, Board of Trustees, University of Illinois.
Reprinted with permission.

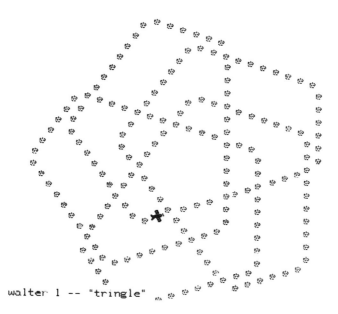

walter 1 -- "tringle"

b

implication), and some work on the relations of mathematics to physical science'' (Davis 1965).

Davis had several reasons for wanting to broaden mathematics education in 1956: (1) ''because concentration on the algorithms of arithmetic is not representative of the mathematics that today's child needs to learn''; (2) ''arithmetic cannot be clearly understood all by itself''; and (3) ''the opportunity for children to *use* arithmetic in creative, original and exciting ways is not great *until* one combines arithmetic with algebra, geometry, and science.'' These statements continue to be strong arguments in favor of school mathematics reform.

In the process of learning these basic ideas of mathematics, acquiring ''mastery of important techniques,'' and knowing ''basic mathematical facts'' the Madison Project also sought to help a student (1) ''develop his ability to discover patterns in abstract situations''; (2) ''develop a habitual use of 'exploratory behavior''' ; and (3) ''acquire a set of mental symbols that will let him think creatively about mathematical situations.'' Furthermore, in noncognitive areas the objectives for the student were: (1) ''a belief that mathematics *is* discoverable''; (2) ''a realistic assessment of one's own ability to discover mathematics''; (3) ''a recognition that mathematics is incomplete and open-ended; there are unexplored frontiers on every side''; (4) ''an honest self-critical ability''; (5) ''an appreciation of—even a commitment to—the value of abstract rational analysis, in its proper place''; (6) ''an appreciation of the value of 'educated intuition' and shrewd speculations''; (7) ''a feeling that mathematics is fun and worthwhile''; (8) ''an appreciation for the history of the development of human culture (in which mathematics has, in fact, played a surprisingly large role)''; and (9) ''an appreciation of pure mathematics for its own sake, together with an appreciation of the scientific uses of mathematics.''

Teachers were expected to grow in the process and to ''live in the world of the child,'' ''in the world of mathematics,'' and in the world of modern adult society. Thus they would ''gain an even deeper understanding of children, and of mathematics, and of the human condition in the twentieth century'' (Davis 1967).

To a great extent, these ideas are incorporated into the Plato Elementary Mathematics Project. The Plato system with its graphics capabilities offered a flexible medium in which to create sets of materials that would provide children with experience in doing mathematics in a creative way through discovery methods. The intention was to help teachers do their job, not to replace them. Thus some of the Plato materials were designed in conjunction with things the teacher would do to prepare children for particular lessons.

The Plato Math Curriculum

The Plato elementary mathematics curriculum, like the CCC math curriculum, is divided into strands, but unlike the CCC materials, which have fourteen strands, Plato math has only three: (1) whole number arithmetic (whole numbers strand); (2) fractions, mixed numbers, and decimals (fractions strand); and (3) graphs, variables, functions, and equations (graphs strand). The strands are made up of lessons and, as pointed out, the lessons vary in style. Some are more didactic than others; some present new ideas; others offer practice in gamelike situations. A typical session lasts about half an hour. A session consists of three slots: (1) a review of previously presented material, (2) main presentation of new lesson, and (3) finally, fun and games. The lessons are presented in a "menu" format and the student selects the lessons.

Davis (1977, pp. 66–67) gives the following overview of the strands:

(1) Whole number arithmetic, including:
meanings of operations
computation techniques and practice
algorithms
place value
renaming and symbols
word problems

(2) Fractions, mixed numbers, and decimals, including:
meanings of fractions and mixed numbers
equivalent fractions
addition, subtraction, and multiplication of fractions
mixed numbers
the meaning of decimal numerals
heuristic approaches to problem solving

(3) Graphs, variables, functions, and equations including:
signed numbers (integers and rationals, positive, negative and zero)
variables and open sentences
exponents
graphs
the representation of functions by graphs, tables, and formulas.

In this curriculum, Davis says "we are recognizing four aspects of mathematical knowledge, and explicitly pursuing three of them" (Davis 1974, p. 171). The four are (Davis 1974, p. 171):

(i) knowing meanings (usually in concrete terms) of various symbols, operations, concepts, etc.

(ii) skill in symbol manipulation

(iii) competence in using heuristic problem-analysis strategies

(iv) having appropriate attitudes and expectations (implicitly dealt with).

The curriculum as implemented on Plato is aimed at fourth, fifth, and sixth graders. The intention is to produce a year's worth of materials for children in these middle grades. The three strands differ in style and content. The whole numbers strand is the largest strand; it is about equivalent to the other two together.

Research on Mathematics Learning

One of Davis's longtime concerns has been the development of research methods that can lead to greater understanding of children's mathematical behavior. Davis finds little use for the abstract / statistical methods prevalent in educational research. "Piaget's clinical interview methodology offers a welcome and important alternative of a radically different type...[with] a relevance guaranteed not by sampling procedures or sample size, but rather by the fundamental nature of the phenomena themselves" (Davis and McKnight 1979, p. 66). Through no fault of Piaget, Davis sees some problems for US Piagetian researchers; for example, "the fundamentals studied by Piaget are relatively remote from typical 'school-type' tasks" and

as Papert has pointed out, the implications of Piaget's results have tended to be reversed in American analysis. Whereas Piaget in fact identified fundamental cognitive abilities that children develop, *even in the absence of formal instruction*, the popular U.S. interpretation reverses this, and contends that Piaget found limitations on a child's "readiness," barriers to what a child is ready to learn. (Davis and McKnight 1979, p. 66)

Davis has collaborated with psychologists, for example, Herbert Ginsburg (Children's Arithmetic), who has been developing observational techniques with children on school-type tasks. More recently, computer scientists and cognitive scientists have been developing theories about human thought processes and forming new conceptualizations of and better ways to talk about children's mathematical behavior. They have done this by providing more powerful images from programming and computer science that researchers can use to discuss and study dynamic processes. Thus there is another way in which Davis thinks about computers. This other way does not use computers to present material but uses the growing body of knowledge developing about thinking, especially by research in artificial intelligence.

Intellectual Background

Davis, in discussing his intellectual influences, cites Polya, Piaget, and Papert. He also acknowledges the influence of MIT and Harvard scientists and mathematicians who interacted through the auspices of Educational Services, Inc. (ESI; now Education Development Corporation (EDC)), started by Jerrold Zacharias and Francis Friedman of MIT. ESI played an important role in the math and science curriculum reforms of the post-Sputnik period, with David Hawkins influencing elementary school science in the form of Elementary Science Study (ESS) materials while Zacharias's Physical Science Study Committee (PSSC) physics for high school students was put into operation. The Cambridge Conference on School Mathematics met through the EDC, chaired by Ted Martin of MIT and Andrew Gleason of Harvard. The elementary math materials of David Page, of the University of Illinois, were also operationalized through ESI. Jerome Bruner, a professor of psychology at Harvard University and a spokesman for developmental psychology in an educational setting, was also a major influence on this group. He tried to articulate a theory of instruction to account for the general approach to education. He also proposed a theory of knowledge that merged Piaget's epistemology, gestalt psychology, Harvard's mainstream psychology (behaviorism), and his colleague George Miller's information processing models. His theory saw knowledge being acquired in three different ways: "enactively" (through actions and thus empirically based), "iconically" (through whole images or gestalts), and "symbolically," as information (Bruner 1966, 44–45). Again we see not one theory but three at work at different stages of a person's development. For Papert and Piaget, this is not the case; they have a consistent account of how knowledge is constructed by children. Bruner's theoretical stance, which attempts to absorb different schools of thought, including behaviorist, gestalt, and information-processing models, has provided cognitive psychologists with an appealing theoretical framework. There is no one theory to account for children's development. Instead there are different theories at different stages of development.

Contributions from Artificial Intelligence

Davis sees the change of focus in the study of mathematics learning now as compared with twenty years ago largely due to the development of

cognitive science, for example, in the work of Minsky, Papert, Schank, Michie, Rumelhart, Ortony, Winograd, and others. In 1960 (or thereabouts) it was commonly argued that "one can't know about what's in people's minds," and hence that the study of learning must deal only with "observable behaviors." Learning itself was commonly defined as a "change in behavior." The interpretation of observable phenomena was cast in terms of real-valued numerical variables, such as I.Q. scores, or various sub-scores on achievement tests.

Opponents of this point of view argued that it represented a distortion of "science," that it did not reflect what one really cares about in the learning of mathematics, and that typical results lacked the specificity that would make them useful for most practical purposes. (Davis and McKnight 1979, p. 94)

Recent studies in mathematics learning "have moved toward answering the main objections that have been leveled against earlier studies. The need for descriptions of more general behavior patterns—identifying bugs in student procedures" as J. S. Brown did in Buggy (Brown and Burton 1977) and "the interpretation of observed behavior in terms of metaphoric models of human information processing" (Davis and McKnight 1979, p. 95).

Implementing the Madison Project on Plato

The elementary school math project came about after the Plato computer system was designed and built. It was part of a national demonstration program to evaluate this computer-based educational system; it was not the reason for the system. Thus the Plato elementary mathematics curriculum came into being in a different way from the CCC materials. A general purpose educational computer was developed separately from particular course content materials (courseware). Plato had gone through significant conceptual development beginning in 1960. It had received considerable funding (in the millions of dollars over the years from the National Science Foundation and from Control Data Corporation (CDC)). Its developers were engineers (D. Alpert and D. Bitzer). Bitzer designed, implemented and patented many innovative hardware components. The goal of building a large computer-based education system capitalizing on graphics terminals for communication between human and computer was largely realized by 1971, and so a national demonstration was called for to evaluate the system's capability.

Plato consists of a CDC computer and Bitzer's plasma panel graphics display terminals with options for micro-fiche projection, for audio output, for touch panel input, and for attachment of other devices. Under Bitzer's supervision the TUTOR programming language had been developed as the machine's language (the chief author was P. Tenzsar). The system during its prior history and development had been used for University of Illinois courses. A new system with plasma panels and TUTOR and ten terminals was operational on a CDC 6500 by January 1972.

The elementary mathematics materials were produced between 1972 and 1976. Originally, the project was to be under the direction of Max Beberman, a mathematics educator at the University of Illinois whose curriculum work had been primarily at the high school level. Beberman died, and in 1972, Bob Davis, then at Syracuse University, was asked to take over both as associate director of the Computer-based Education Research Laboratory (CERL) in charge of the elementary mathematics project and also as director of the Curriculum Laboratory. Davis was thus responsible for the running of University High School, a school that sought talented students in the Champaign-Urbana area.

Davis began assembling a team of people to develop materials. He brought two of his Madison Project staff members with him. The others were primarily graduate students or undergraduate students at the University of Illinois. Although longtime members of the CERL staff made contributions (Esther Steinberg contributed eight lessons to the Whole Numbers Strand; six other lessons in that strand were developed by other CERL staff), there was a changeover as Davis's philosophy of instruction began to be implemented (Seiler and Weaver 1976). Many of the new CERL members had no prior experience with Plato, but they had backgrounds in mathematics education.

Some Criticisms of the Madison Project on Plato

One of the tasks of the Madison Project was "to devise suitable 'process' experiences, and to give teachers the necessary educational background to cope with the demands of this style of teaching" (Davis 1967b, vol. 1, p. 46). Now the task was to find "process" experiences that would utilize Plato, graphics, touch input, etc. and that could be implemented on Plato, preserving the Madison Project style of teaching. The Davis group anticipated developing materials in a style similar to the way Madison Project materials evolved:

The procedure was developed of having a team of mathematically-competent people and educationally-sophisticated people work out a flexible and tentative lesson plan, try it out with children, discuss it, revise it and polish it, subject it to further trials, and—when it seemed to be in reasonably stable shape—*teach it to children to whom it was a new lesson and record the interplay between teacher and children on film, video-tape, or audiotape.* (Davis 1967b, vol. 1, p. 47)

The immediacy of the national demonstration, only two years from the inception of the project, and the style imposed by the Educational Testing Service evaluators created conditions under which the material could not be revised even though actual experience in the classroom indicated places for revision.

Each strand and the lessons within the strands called for different kinds of change. Perhaps no one was more aware of the need for a second pass on implementing elementary mathematics in the style of the Madison Project than Davis. There were several factors that impeded revision. After the demonstration, research funding to Plato was drastically reduced. The commercial costs of Plato itself were too high to support its use in schools. Bitzer anticipated costcutting by using cable or broadcast bands instead of telephone lines, but the FCC withheld its approval at that time. Thus the impetus to revise the materials was missing. Furthermore, the authors retained individual ownership of the lessons they wrote. When funding was cut, so were their jobs. They did not want to see their materials changed.

Nonetheless, the evolution of the three strands and their lessons makes an interesting story in the development of educational software. The three strands were under the general direction of Davis but were designed and implemented by three groups of people. The Fractions Strand was authored primarily by Sharon Dugdale and David Kibbey, who had been students at Illinois. The Graphs Strand authors were Donald Cohen and Gerald Glynn, who had been Madison Project staff members. The Whole Numbers Strand had been begun with material prepared before Davis's arrival. Eventually the major authors were Bonnie Seiler and Charles Weaver. Seiler was a graduate student at Illinois. Her first Plato program was West. As a result of this piece of work Seiler joined the staff and became a coauthor of the strand.

The Whole Numbers Strand offers the most diversity in instructional style, in lessons, and in games, drills, and didactics. Although West is outstanding, the Whole Numbers Strand does not maintain this quality of spirit and content throughout. Initially, the children thought that the Whole Numbers Strand was the most fun with Speedway, Parking Lot, Egg Factory, Home Sweet Toadstool, Hockey, and Wheel of Fortune. But the lessons quickly became boring to advanced fifth and sixth graders. The Fractions Strand on the other hand was more didactic and structured in teaching style. Serious shortcomings of the Fractions Strand are its intensity of purpose and its compactness. If there were more themes to choose from, then perhaps its relentless teaching could be less intense. Instead, it has a reputation among its child users of being less fun than the other strands (Davis 1980). The Graphs Strand closely follows the Madison Project materials, such as postman stories, "Guess My Rule," and the tower of Hanoi puzzle. The presentation is wordy and makes less use of "graphics" than the other strands. This strand was too advanced for many fourth graders.

Davis's Plato Math and Microcomputers

CDC, who began to market Plato commercially, had the option to promote this elementary math program but chose instead to push basic skills material (generated for use in community colleges) in the style of the CCC materials. (CDC was planning its nationwide network of learning centers and saw competency-based education in the form of drill-and-practice materials as a strong selling feature.) The CDC decision to set up learning centers might have been an important educational step. Unfortunately, the materials were not innovative, as Davis's were. The materials imitated CCC's but did not have the early research cycles in which to debug the material. Moreover, the microcomputer boom changed people's expectations. If they went to a center outside of school, then they wanted to learn to use a computer that they could also use at home. The centers were not economically viable, but CDC's founder, William Norris, has a deep commitment to education, and CDC is still pursuing the Plato dream. Plato terminals have been transformed into stand-alone systems, but they do not have a significant educational following. More recently, CDC entered a venture with CAI enthusiasts in Utah (WICAT) to develop curricula for schools using computer and videodisk technology. Theoretically, this group is closer to Suppes than to Davis with their behaviorist approach to learning.[1] The theoretical foundations contrast with those of Davis. Discovery learning is replaced by rote learning. It is unlikely that CDC will review Davis's contributions and take advantage of them.

Davis's Plato math materials have been available only to users with access to the University of Illinois's system. In the late 1970s, a diverse population gained access through time-shared connections. But the materials have been difficult to transport to school microcomputers such as Apple IIs and IBM PCs because of the low resolution of their graphics. Math lessons, such as West, Darts, and Share Jumping Beans, take advantage of the high resolution graphics and text intermix of the Plato screen. The educational impact of integrating visual images into an interactive textbook owes its proof of concept to Bitzer, Davis and others at the University of Illinois. Imaginative integration of graphic images and subject matter demonstrates the possibility of creating discovery-learning environments with a computer. This use of graphics is different from putting a little smiling face on a graphics screen whenever the user gets the right answer to a question and replacing the smile with a frown when a wrong answer is entered.

Davis had hoped to redesign the lessons completely. This would have required extensive funding and thus never happened. Nonetheless, many of his lessons have served as models to the present generation of software developers in the microcomputer explosion. Microcomputer software, such as the materials of the Learning Company (from Juggle's Rainbow to Rocky's Boots), are examples of integrated graphical learning environments set up to teach particular concepts. Using graphics and sound, Juggle's Rainbow teaches preschoolers about the concepts above, below, left, and right. Rocky's Boots, a much more ambitious undertaking, teaches digital logic design by having the user explore different learning environments and build different logic systems out of wires and logic gates.

At this point, however, there is no new research endeavor on the order of Davis's to create a discovery-learning environment for elementary school mathematics. Let's hope that a new group of talented researchers dedicated to children's cognitive and social development will undertake the development of materials of this quality and that they will build in enough time to test the materials with children and to revise them.

4

Dwyer: Eclecticism and Heuristic Learning

We have seen that compared with Suppes, Davis has a less rigid approach to instruction and a broader sense of what constitutes mathematical knowledge. Nevertheless, his model of mathematics is firmly defined, and his learning experiences are purposefully designed to lead the child to a small, well-defined set of classical "powerful" ideas, such as variable and function, and induction of rules. We move next to a much more eclectic approach presently being carried vigorously into schools by the wave of low-priced microcomputers.)

Microcomputers gave a new impetus to computing activities in education as the number of people who could obtain access to computers burgeoned. Microcomputers attracted a wide variety of users including hobbyists, home consumers looking for personal ways to use computers, and teachers and students exploring direct educational applications. This wide and diverse base of users gave a grass roots quality to the early phases of this growing computer culture. There was also a general feeling that computers would contribute not only to mathematics learning but also to every other area of one's intellectual life, in addition to opening new career opportunities. But perhaps the dominant feeling within this community of users is that now anyone can do what previously only a few people in research laboratories could do.

Typically, a microcomputer system consists of a keyboard, a TV set, and the BASIC programming language. It might have a tape recorder or a floppy disk drive for permanent storage of programs and data as well as a printer for listing programs and computations. BASIC was the first and is often the only language other than the machine instructions available to the computer. This language influenced activities in this growing culture. It also provided direct links with previous work in computers and education. Researchers, such as Tom Dwyer, explored the possibilities of interactive computing using the BASIC language.

In fact, workers from two different areas of computers and education jumped on the microcomputer bandwagon: those who believe that the best way to use computers is to have the computer control the student and those who believe that the best way to use the computer is to have students control the computer. Nonetheless, the dominant attitude within the BASIC culture is to teach students to program and to have them use some prepared materials, especially simulations. The eclectic nature of the BASIC culture is one of its most appealing aspects and at the same time one of its inhibiting characteristics.

BASIC and microcomputers together have given rise to a particular computer culture, which I refer to as the BASIC computer culture. There are many facets to this culture and many enthusiastic and active supporters. There is no one spokesperson, no one central figure who has given it shape. Of the several possible representatives of this culture I choose Tom Dwyer as an example. His views and theoretical position seem to reflect the dreams and aspirations of this diverse culture.

An Overview

Dwyer wants to reform the process of teaching and learning. He sees computers as providing a way to achieve this reformation. Dwyer shares with Seymour Papert, Alan Kay, and others (including me) the belief that the best computer learning experiences consist of learning to master the computer. We will see that he differs from Papert and Kay in his model of what constitutes mastery of the computer and what needs to be done to achieve it.

I have introduced into my discussion of the theorists discussed so far some elements from their personal lives. With Dwyer, a significant element is his involvement in flying. Dwyer is a pilot, and flying is an important part of his mental imagery. Dwyer's central model for learning is derived from this involvement. The crucial moment in learning to fly is the dramatic first solo. The goal of initial instruction for the fledgling pilot is to reach the degree of proficiency needed for solo learning, in which the pilot flies out alone, taking charge of his or her own learning. Dwyer is struck by this quality of the computer: The learner-programmer comes more quickly to the stage of solo learning than in most other fields.

The realization of Dwyer's dream of solo learning is shaped by another personal attribute: He is a man of action. In the 1960s Papert and Kay were dreaming of how children would program the computers of the 1980s and 1990s. Dwyer wanted them programming the machines available right then and using the programming languages available right then. This commit-

ment to action determined a major thrust of his work: how to use the BASIC
language in an educationally meaningful way.

A final major difference that sets Dwyer apart from Suppes and Davis is
his grass roots origin in classroom teaching. For the others, "teaching" has
meant teaching in elite universities with an occasional foray into schools.
Before Dwyer became a professor of computer science, he was a high
school teacher, and this background shows itself in a particularly respectful
attitude toward the teacher. The thrust of Suppes's work is to eliminate the
teacher. Davis seeks to define the teacher's role in the form of well-worked-
out scripts. Dwyer recommends a mode of instruction that is, in his own
words, "harder on the teacher than on the student." And, generally, one
finds more references to the role of the teacher and models of the teaching
process in Dwyer's writings that in the writings of the others.

At the core of Dwyer's approach to using computers is the idea of giving
the student mastery of the computer: The student should program the computer and use it as an instrument for music and for graphic arts, as a
simulator for learning to fly airplanes, as a physics or mathematics
laboratory, and so on. The educational value of doing this is bolstered by
reference to a list of "educational theorists, including Aristotle, Aquinas,
Whitehead, Dewey, and Piaget, on the writings of psychologists like Rogers
and Maslow, and on some of the contemporary insights of people like Illich
and Papert" (Dwyer 1974, p. 138). From these thinkers Dwyer sees a common view of education as *"that which liberates human potential, and thus
the person"* (Dwyer 1974, p. 138).

Dwyer (1974, p. 138) sees education as "helping people achieve certain
kinds of control over their lives"—a "liberating control" that extends not
only to the environment in social, physical, and economic aspects but also
to themselves, contributing to "internal" control or self-control; and he sees
computers in education as a way of creating a learning environment where
this can occur, where learning to control a computer connects with all
aspects of people's lives.

The Teaching Process

Dwyer wants to reform the process of teaching and learning. His vision of
what is possible is based on his personal experiences in flying airplanes, in
programming computers, and in teaching high school. From his flying experiences he captures a metaphor explaining his theory of education: dual
mode and solo mode learning. He takes as his model of a teacher a flying
instructor whose goal is to "transmit" enough information and experience
to his or her students while they are together, in dual mode, to enable the

students to solo, to fly alone successfully. Success is determined not by a test but by not crashing and not causing others to crash.

The teacher and the student form a relationship, which Dwyer formalizes. It is a relationship that is a celebration of "good teaching." The teacher's role is to convey information and "sensitize" the student into "receiving" the information. Doing this requires active participation by teacher and student. This dual participation becomes clear in learning to fly. The student and the teacher *know* they are working toward the same end—getting the student to fly by herself. This process requires the student to internalize for herself flying knowledge and experiences. When the student is soloing she is on her own and must rely on what she knows and on debugging techniques developed while under the direct influence of her teacher.

The teacher *knows* that the student must "appropriate" flying knowledge for herself, and so the teacher must also be a sensitive transmitter and know that it is impossible to impose her own structure on the student. The instructor's job is to help the student construct her own mental models of how to fly. There will, of course, be shared metaphors, but, whether these mental constructs are identical or different, this constructivist view of the teaching process is particularly conducive to a programming environment.

This view puts the student in control and indeed turns the teacher into a facilitator. Then discussion about teaching and learning styles takes on a different complexion. Whether it is more optimal for a student to use a drill-and-practice routine or a scripted discovery-learning routine can now be tested in a different way because it is with the student's consent and participation that one method is chosen over another, if either is chosen. Once the student is in control of her own learning, both the teacher and the student are working toward a common goal: liberating the student to reach her potential through education.

Examples of Programming in BASIC

Dwyer's vision of what can happen to students and teachers in a supportive learning environment has been shared by many teachers and students who have themselves learned to program computers,. To show what it means for a young beginning student to program computers I begin with some examples of the most elementary kinds of program and proceed from there to progressively more complex examples. I have, however, taken some liberties in my selection and have chosen some examples from my own work with children in Logo classes in the 1960s. At that time, uppercase typewriter terminals were used as input devices to time-shared computers. These Logo examples circulated among many educational computerists in-

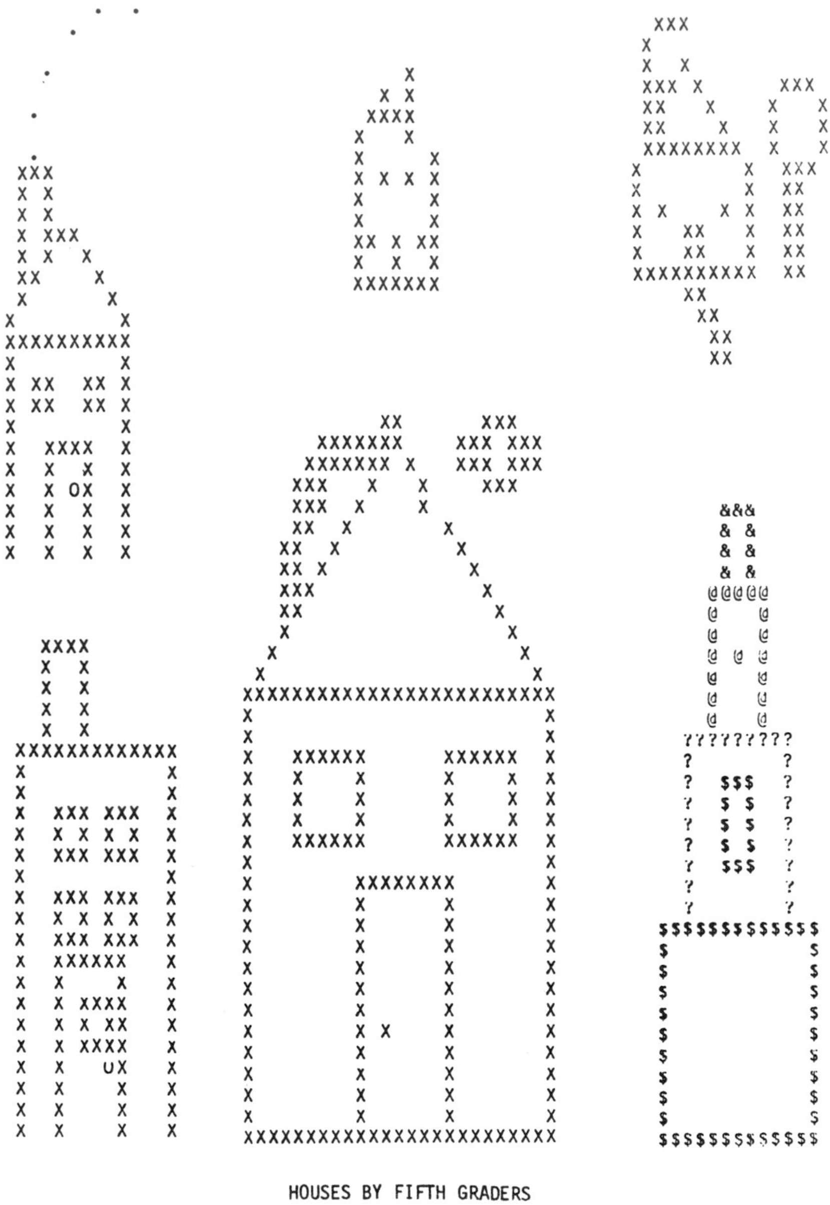

HOUSES BY FIFTH GRADERS

Figure 4.1
Examples of designs that can be made in BASIC (originally written in Logo).

cluding those using BASIC. Before then, typical introductory sessions involved children writing programs to find the average of five numbers. Unfortunately, writing the program was more complicated than solving the problem by hand. Furthermore, the computer did not provide the child with a deeper insight into the problem.

An excellent introductory activity involves graphing; the student writes programs to print keyboard characters in planned patterns. Graphical representations include houses, dogs, people, signs, and words. The programs which generate these figures are remarkably close to the figures themselves, thus acquiring a kind of concreteness that makes them a good first step into programming. The programming style of using PRINT statements in BASIC to make a picture is similar to Logo techniques. For example:

```
Program                          Result

10 PRINT "DDD        D"      DDD        D
20 PRINT "DDDD       D"      DDDD       D
30 PRINT "   DDDDDDDD"       DDDDDDDD
40 PRINT "   D D  D D"       D D  D D
50 PRINT "   D D  D D"       D D  D D
60 PRINT "   D D  D D"       D D  D D
70 PRINT "11111111111"       11111111111111
80 END
```

Other examples of figures made in this way (Papert and Solomon 1971, pp. 27–29) are shown in figure 4.1.

For beginners in BASIC, a typical direction to take after graphing pictures is generating tables of numbers using a FOR...NEXT loop. For example (Dwyer and Critchfield 1978, p. 18):

```
10 PRINT "MULT. TABLE FOR 9"
20 FOR K=0 TO 12
30 PRINT K*9
40 NEXT K
50 END
```

```
RUN

MULT. TABLE FOR 9
0
9
18
27
36
45
54
63
72
81
90
99
108
OK
```

Children like playing with words and sentences, and in Logo they might continue this theme. For example, a typical Logo project in the 1960s involved some kind of wordplay. In the following example, a child made up lists of nouns, verbs, adjectives, determiners, and so on. She then used a previously defined procedure to *pick* a word from a list (Papert and Solomon 1971, p. 28).

```
THE FUNNY PROF TALKED WHILE THAT COOL KID KISSED...
SOME FUNNY PROF WALKED BUT A BEAUTIFUL KID CLAPED...
A WILD DONKEY KISSED WHILE THE FUNNY PROF CLAPED...
SOME GROSS PROF WALKED ALTHOUGH SOME COOL KID HUMMED...
```

Here are the procedures:

```
TO SENGEN
SIMPLE.SEN
TYPE PICK [BUT WHILE ALTHOUGH]
SIMPLE.SEN
PRINT []
END
```

```
TO SIMPLE.SEN
TYPE PICK [THAT THE A SOME]
TYPE PICK [COOL WILD GROSS BEAUTIFUL]
TYPE PICK [DONKEY PROF KID]
TYPE PICK [WALKED CLAPED KISSED HUMMED WALKED]
END
```

Although this project might have been written by a ten-year-old in Logo, in BASIC it would have been too difficult. BASIC was designed to manipulate numbers not words.

The following project (Dwyer and Critchfield 1978, p. 161), which follows a template made up by the programmer, is easier to write in BASIC but would probably be undertaken by a junior or senior high school student.

```
10 PRINT"THIS PROGRAM CAN HELP YOU BECOME A
'POET'."
20 PRINT"PLEASE TYPE IN THE FOLLOWING KINDS OF
WORDS OR PHRASES"
30 PRINT"AS THE PROGRAM ASKS FOR THEM:"
40 PRINT"NOUN—";:INPUT N$
50 PRINT"ADJECTIVE DESCRIBING THE NOUN—";:INPUT A$
60 PRINT"ANOTHE ADJECTIVE—";:INPUT A$
70 PRINT"A PREPOSITIONAL PHRASE TELLING"
75 PRINT"WHERE OR WHEN SOMETHING CAN HAPPEN TO YOUR
NOUN—";:INPUT P$
80 PRINT"A VERB—";:INPUT V$
90 PRINT"AN ADVERB DESCRIBING HOW YOUR NOUN DOES
IT—";:INPUT C$
95 PRINT"ANOTHER ADVERB—";:INPUT D$
100 PRINT"HERE IS THE 'POEM':":PRINT
110 PRINT"THE ";N$
120 PRINT" ";A$;", ";B$
130 PRINT P$
140 PRINT" ";C$;", ";D$
150 PRINT V$;"."
155 PRINT
160 PRINT"WANT TO MAKE ANOTHER 'POEM'";:INPUT Z$
170 IF Z$="YES" THEN 40
180 END
```

```
RUN

THIS PROGRAM CAN HELP YOU BECOME A 'POET'.
PLEASE TYPE IN THE FOLLOWING KINDS OF WORDS OR
PHRASES
AS THE PROGRAM ASKS FOR THEM:
NOUN—? SNOW
ADJECTIVE DESCRIBING THE NOUN—? GRAY
ANOTHER ADJECTIVE—? RAGGED
A PREPOSITIONAL PHRASE TELLING
WHERE OR WHEN SOMETHING CAN HAPPEN TO YOUR NOUN—?
BETWEEN THE BUILDINGS
A VERB—? FALLS
AN ADVERB DESCRIBING HOW YOUR NOUN DOES IT—?
SLOWLY
ANOTHER ADVERB—? UNCERTAINLY

HERE IS THE 'POEM':

THE SNOW
          GRAY, RAGGED
BETWEEN THE BUILDINGS
          SLOWLY, UNCERTAINLY
FALLS.

WANT TO MAKE ANOTHER 'POEM'? NO
```

Children like developing CAI programs, such as interactive mathematical sentence generators. We are reminded here of Suppes, but in this case the children create their own drills. The first example of this kind of work occurred in a Logo class from 1968 to 1969. Nonetheless, children later developed this style of project in BASIC because it involves numbers and not words. Children might start such a project by printing the generated sentence. Later, they modify the program so that it asks a user to supply the answer. They then concentrate on responding to the user.

The effect is something like

$7 + 4 = 11$
$3 + 2 = 5$
$9 + 6 = 15$

and so on. A slight modification will cause the computer to print something like

$7 + 4 = ?$

and wait for a human victim to type something in order to insult him if he fails to give the appropriate answer. For example:

```
7 + 4 = ?                        (Computer)
ELEVEN                           (Victim)
IDIOT, THE ANSWER IS 11          (Computer)
```

Even when the [program] has been modified to accept "ELEVEN" we can still tease the victim:

```
7 + 4 = ?

ELEVEN

DON'T THINK YOU ARE SMART, YOU TOOK MORE THAN
   2 SECONDS.
```

(Papert and Solomon 1971, p. 30)

Other popular programming projects are games such as NIM, which involves modular arithmetic, and word games based on Hangman. Again I have taken the liberty of selecting examples from my experiences with Logo classes as well as from Dwyer's repertoire. The projects as developed in Logo could be implemented by children younger than those who develop such projects in BASIC.

NIM

```
DO YOU KNOW HOW TO PLAY NIM?
<NO
HERE ARE THE RULES: YOU WILL BE SHOWN A COLLEC-
TION OF X'S.
YOU MAY REMOVE 1, 2, OR 3. THE PLAYER WHO TAKES
THE LAST X WINS.
THIS IS PROBABLY TOO VAGUE FOR YOU TO UNDERSTAND,
BUT TRY PLAYING AND
I'LL CORRECT YOUR MISTAKES.

ARE YOU READY?
<I AM
OK. NOW TELL ME THE NAME OF THE FIRST PLAYER.
<JON
NOW THE NAME OF THE OTHER PLAYER
<COMPUTER
HOW MANY STICKS DO YOU WANT TO START WITH?
```

```
<THIRTY-ONE
I'M A DUMB COMPUTER. TYPE A PROPER NUMERAL.
<31

JON TO PLAY.
THERE ARE 31 STICKS.
XXXXXXXXXXXXXXXXXXXXXXXXXXXXXXX
JON, TAKE 1, 2, OR 3
<3

COMPUTER TO PLAY.
THERE ARE 28 STICKS.
XXXXXXXXXXXXXXXXXXXXXXXXXXXX
I TAKE 3

JON TO PLAY.
THERE ARE 25 STICKS.
XXXXXXXXXXXXXXXXXXXXXXXXX
JON, TAKE 1, 2, OR 3
<3
 .
 .
 .
```

(Papert and Solomon 1970b, p. 14)

Here is Dwyer's version of Hangman (Dwyer and Critchfield 1978, p. 166; © 1978, Addison-Wesley. Reprinted with permission):

```
RUN
WORD GUESSING GAME
IF YOU GET 8 WRONG GUESSES, THE NOSTER WILL EAT
YOU!
WANT MONSTER TO BE VISIBLE? YES


 _____

GUESS A LETTER? E
SORRY,NOT IN WORD.
(( ))
( ** ** )
LETTERS YOU USED:
E
```

———

```
GUESS A LETTER? A

———A—

GUESS THE WORD?
NO—TRY ANOTHER LETTER
LETTERS YOU USED:
E,A

-A———A—

GUESS A LETTER? I
SORRY,NOT IN WORD.
(( ))
( ** ** )
** * **
LETTERS YOU USED:
E,A,I

-A———A—

GUESS A LETTER? T
SORRY,NOT IN WORD.
(( ))
( ** ** )
** * **
* *
LETTERS YOU USED:
E,A,I,T

-A———A—

GUESS A LETTER? O

-A—OA—

GUESS THE WORD? PAYLOAD
RIGHT!!! YOU TOOK 5 GUESSES.
WANT ANOTHER WORD
```

? NO
SO LONG.

These ideas lead to other more-complex programming projects that elementary school children often *use* rather than write. For example, in Lemonade the user pretends to run a lemonade stand and, within the constraints of the program's economic model, makes a profit or suffers a financial loss. The user is asked to price the lemonade and to specify the amount, and the computer does the rest.

Finally, there are some examples of elaborate design plotting programs (figure 4.2).

History of Project Solo

Project Solo began in 1969. Terminals connected to a time-shared computer were placed in a large high school. The project concentrated on preparing curriculum materials, developing courses for teachers, and providing expertise on technical issues. From 1972 to 1977, Dwyer ran the Soloworkers Laboratory Project. In this new research phase, the laboratory extended its concerns of interactive computing to exploring various input/output devices including "computer-controlled robots, lunar landers, a computer-controlled pipe organ, a flight simulator, plotters, and color graphics" (Dwyer and Critchfield 1982, p. 8). In 1980 the Solo/NET/works Project began; this project extends the previous work by developing a microcomputer network and software for "running role-playing simulations" and letting users "write their own multi-process simulations" so that the "system could support inventive pedagogies as well as inventive learning" (Dwyer and Critchfield 1982, p. 8).

Although Project Solo work has focused primarily on junior and senior high school students and college students, its use of computers in education has influenced computing activities in elementary schools now, with individual teachers introducing computers to their students as "personal intellectual tools." The microcomputer has enhanced this possibility of computers becoming personal tools because computer costs have decreased. Because most microcomputers come equipped with the BASIC programming language, a bit of BASIC's and Project Solo's histories might shed some light on current activities.

The Project Solo view of computers extends the tradition begun at Dartmouth College, where BASIC was developed in a time-sharing environment in the 1960s. There, every calculus student learned to write six programs in BASIC. John Kemeny, then head of Dartmouth's math depart-

```
3333            4444444444444444444444444                4444444444444444444444444              3333
333      44444               444444444444444444444444               444444        333
33     4444        555555555          44444444444444444444              55555        4444     33
3      444      555         5555       44444444444444444       5555          5555    4444      3
       444    55  666666666    555      444444444444       555   66666666    555   4444
     444  55   6   77   77  66   555      44444444       555   6   777777   66 55   444
    444  55  6   78  9999 8 7 6   55       444444      55  6   7 8 999 8 7 6   5    444
    444   5 6 7      <  <      7 6  55       444444      55 6 7   9:;<<<;:98   6 55    44
    44  55 6      ;  @ DC@      7 6  55       444444      5  6      ;=@ D @=;  87 6 5    44
    44  55 6789  =        A= 987 6 55       444444      5  67 9     V JV         6 5    44
    444 55 67 9  =         = 987 6 5       444444444    55 6     :      V JVG  :   6 5   44
     44   5 6   8  ;=@ D @=;      6 55       44444      4444    55 6789  = B B = 9876 5    44      3
    3    444 55 6  89:;  <  ;:98  6 55    444           444 55 67          76 55  44     333
   33    444 55 6 7 88     88 66 5  444           333        44  5  6 7 888   7 6 5   44     333
  333    444  55 66        6  5   444      333333333333    44  5  66666    55  44      3333
 33333    444    55         555  44   33333       333   444       444    33333
 333333    444              444   333      222222222      333        33333
  333333      444444       3333   22222     1111111111      222222 3333333333
    333333333       333333   22222    1111111111      11111       222222            22222
         333333333    2222   11111            11111     2222222222222
2222              222222   1111   00000          00000   11111              22222
222222222222222222222222     111    000   //////////  000    11111
222222222222222222        1111   000  ///   ....   ....  ///   000    11111
                   11111   00   //   ..    --        --  ..  //  000   111111
            111111    000   //   .  -  ,  ++     ++ ,  -- .  /   000   111111
         111111111    0000   //   .  -  , *)(  )   ) + ,- .. //  00     11111
       111111111111   0000   //  . - ,   *)('&%    &   +, - . // 00      1111
11111111111111111    0000   ///  .. - ,    $-     $& )*+, - . /   000      1111
11111111111111     000000   ///  .  -  *   *  *    #  )  ,- . //  00       111
1111111      0000000   ///   .  -  ,+  ( $!       !  '*+,  . /   00        111
111     0000000    ////  .. -- ,+*)(&$!     !  '*+,  . /   00        111
1      00000000    /////  .. , ,+  '%      #  )  ,- . //  00        1111
     00000000    /////   ... -- , +#)('      '$& )*+,  . /  00        1111
    0000000    ///////   ... - , +*    &%    &    +, . /  000       11111
   000000    ///////    ....  -- , * )  ((( )  +, - . //  00      111111
  000000    //////    .....     -- , ++     ++ , - . /  00     111111
 00000   /////     ............     --- ,,,,, -- .. // 000    111111
 0000   /////   ................     --- .. / 00  11111
 00    ////  ...                    ....... ...........    // 00 11     2222222
 0   ///  ... --          ----    /// 00 1 22        222222222
 0   ///  .. -- ,,     ,, --   ....   /////   00 1 22 3 4444   333     22222
 ///  . - ,+ **  * +,, - ...     ///  00 1 2 3 4   66 5 44 33       22
 //  .. - ,     *+ , - ..  ///   00 1 23 456789   76 44 333        2
 //  . - ,    )*+, - .. //    000 11 2 3    =@ @ ;9   5 4 333
 ///  . - ,+*(&       ( + - .. ///  00 11 ?  0568 >EThT  , 765 4  333
 ///  , - ,+*(@      d( + - .. //  000  1  2 3 45 8    Th    ; 76  44 333
 //  . -,  ) # # )  , - .. //   00 11  2 345679;> B > 8 65 44 333
 //  .. - ,    , - .. //    00  11 22 3 4 56789: :    6 5 4  333
 ///  .. - ,+  *** + - .. //  000  111 22 3 4 5 6 7777 6 5 4     333
 ///  .. -  ,,, ,,, - . ///  000  11  22 33 44 55    55 44  333
 0   ///  -------  .. ///  0000  11  22 33 444    444  3333
 00   ///  .....  ... ///  0000  111  222  33          33333
 000   /////   ////  0000   111  222   333333333333333
 00000   //////////////   0000   11111   2222   333333333
 0000000    ////////   00000   11111   22222             2
  000000000    000000   111111   222222           222222
  00000000000000    000000000   111111   222222222222   2222222222
  00000000000000000000000   111111   222222222222222222222222
   0000000000000000000   1111111   22222222222222222222222
      00000   11111111   222222222222222222222
               1111111111   2222222222222222222222
                1111111111   222222222222222222222
```

a

Figure 4.2

Elaborate designs made by using more complex BASIC plotting programs (Dwyer and Critchfield 1978, pp. 306–308; © 1978, Addison-Wesley. Reprinted with permission).

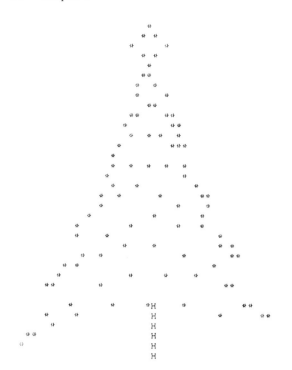

Figure 4.2 *b*

RUN

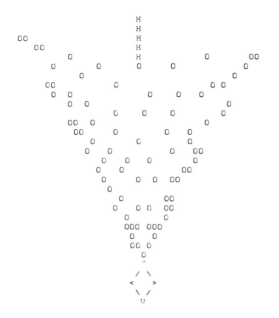

ment along with Tom Kurtz, designed BASIC specifically to serve the needs of Dartmouth students in this era preceding the availability of microprocessor based hand-held calculators (Kemeny and Kurtz 1967). Project Solo carries the image of computers as personal tools beyond the calculus or algebra classroom to everyone interested in learning to use computers. In schools today this appeal is echoed by many of the active computer users who want to go "beyond CAI" (Critchfield 1979, p. 18). But the model of the project initially follows a pattern of other projects of the 1960s involving high school students, for example, at Bolt, Beranek and Newman, using TELCOMP, and at Dartmouth, using BASIC. Dwyer, who joined the young computer science department of the University of Pittsburgh in 1968, initiated Project Solo shortly thereafter under a grant from the National Science Foundation. Project Solo then involved three high schools in the greater Pittsburgh area.

This and subsequent projects carried on by other researchers in other parts of the country either offered in-service workshops during the year or ran summer institutes for teachers, in which the teachers would learn to program in an algebraic language. In the fall following the summer institute, a number of terminals would be installed in the high schools and the teachers would then use them to enhance and supplement their regular math or science curricula. The project staff would make on site visits, run in-service workshops, observe the classes, make suggestions, help to prepare materials (new programming projects), explain new programming ideas, etc. The teachers and their students were major collaborators in the project initiating programs of their own out of their own interests. The games, simulations, etc. that owe their origin to high school teachers and students are considerable (See Ahl, *101 BASIC Computer Games* and Braun's Huntington I materials as examples.)

These, like so many other research projects, tend to attract and involve the "top" teachers and the "top" students, although anecdotes abound about mediocre students who are fired up by the computer's presence. Nonetheless, students under the influence of these computing environments do things they would not otherwise do. This immediate and dramatic demonstration of student productivity and creativity reinforces Dwyer's view that computer technology offers a heuristic methodology for "liberating the human potential, and thus the person."

These projects demonstrate that the computer under human control is a potentially powerful human tool. It can be used in a variety of ways for different purposes. This potential can be realized by anyone, not only by experts at universities or in industry. What is needed is to put the tool in the hands of the people and then to give the people suggestions of things that have already been done. Out of these programs the people will create new ones for their own personal use or will reappropriate some of those created by others for their own personal amusement, edification, and pleasure.

Theory and Practice: An Inherent Contradiction

Up to this point I have concentrated on presenting Dwyer's attractive educational philosophy. I turn next to a discussion of some of the difficulties of the task of implementing these ideas. In doing this, I have tried to avoid *ad hoc* criticisms and concentrate on a fundamental and almost universal dilemma of educational innovation. The innovator tends to be—and Dwyer certainly is—action oriented. But reality sets a trap for the revolutionary activist: The most utopian visions of the future can be undermined when the means to achieve them are borrowed from the systems they wish to replace. Dwyer himself warns of this danger:

attempting to innovate with supportive systems that don't begin to match the sophistication of the human learner should be viewed as a betrayal, not a consequence, of a humanistic approach to education. (Dwyer 1971a, p. 100)

But I believe that Dwyer falls into a fundamental inconsistency in failing to take his own advice: By adopting the easily available BASIC as the computer language, he undermines his own utopian vision. Understanding how this happens requires a closer look at the large community of BASIC users and at the language itself.

BASIC and Its Community

As microcomputers equipped with BASIC began to find their way into people's lives, there was an increased sense of personal power to turn the computer into a tool for work and play. A proliferation of magazines and primers appeared in bookstores, on newstands, and in computer stores directed at this wide community of users, telling them what they could do and how they could get started. Most of these magazines and books described programs written in BASIC. Educational software packages made available for the new generation of computers was often written in BASIC. These software packages ranged from drill-and-practice materials in the style of Suppes to lessons derived from Plato-like materials. There was also a large number of simulations and games developed by teachers, researchers, and children in various BASIC programming environments.

Some of the people behind the primers, programs, and other published materials available by 1980 have been outspoken advocates of computers in education since the 1960s, when they used BASIC on time-shared computers. Another common element in this culture was (at least theoretically) a feeling that the ideas and programs—the materials, the courseware—were created or could be created by teachers in the field and students in the classroom or at home. (For example, Ahl's *101 BASIC Computer Games*, an annotated collection of programs, many of which were written by high school students. The most popular programs in the collection, Hamurabi and Lunar Lander were written by Ahl (1973, 1978).)

Other Activists in the BASIC Culture

I would like to mention some other people who have been outspoken advocates of computing activities in schools: Ludwig Braun, Bob Albrecht, David Ahl, and Arthur Luehrmann.

Ludwig Braun, a professor at the New York Institute of Technology, became known to the education world when he developed a series of simulation materials (Huntington I and II) in the late 1960s and early 1970s. The Huntington Computer Project began while Braun was at the Polytechnic Institute of Brooklyn and was funded by the National Science Foundation. The project engaged high school students in developing and using simulation programs written in BASIC for biology, chemistry, earth science, mathematics, and social studies. These materials were widely distributed by Digital Equipment Corporation to run on their PDP-8 (the educational computer of the 1970s). The Huntington materials were used extensively in junior and senior high schools (Huntington Computer Project 1971).

A typical example of the Huntington simulations is POLUT, a program on water pollution. In this program the user can vary five different parameters: the kind of body of water, the water temperature, the kind of waste, the rate at which the waste is dumped per day into the water, and the type of treatment of the waste. The parameter options are well defined; the program does not have to make theories. It computes a table of figures and / or a graph displaying for each day the oxygen content and the waste content of the water until the conditions become stable and there are no new observable effects.

Braun contrasts sharply with Dwyer in the extent to which his writing emphasizes the technology as such rather than the principles of educational philosophy. Braun is a "technologist"; he sees computers as *the* advanced technology of the information age we live in and believes deeply in their capacity to be harnessed to improve educational productivity. He talks about how student dropout rates will decrease and student test scores will increase as computers provide instruction and attention for individual students. He believes in using computers to improve education in traditionally measurable ways through standardized testing. He is not challenging the ongoing educational enterprise but rather seeking ways to deliver it. He is currently developing CAI materials on personal computers for standard high school algebra (Braun 1980).

Braun shares with Dwyer a belief in the computer and a sense of immediacy—of using computers and programming languages that are available now. Like Dwyer, he believes that the computer can potentially meet the diverse needs of teachers and students and that doing so requires developing materials. The first difference between them is seen in their ideas of what constitutes "materials." Braun's materials are tightly defined and clearly related to specific traditional subject matter. Dwyer's "materials" tend to be environments in which students take their own paths. This difference is rooted in their respective views of educational philosophy. Dwyer sees the computer as a way of liberating people to reach their potential in a humanistic tradition based on realizing one's own creative powers through learning to control and not be controlled by computers. Braun takes a more technocratic view of using computers to educate people according to current societal demands.

Braun, like Suppes, recognizes the impact of computers on his own intellectual life. For example, in his public presentations he talks about the positive effects on him, a nonmusician, of his own computer-generated music programs. But, like Suppes, he does not see that sharing these experiences with thousands of students and teachers is either possible or practical with respect to cost and productivity. Thus in his proselytizing Braun appears to be a revolutionary—he wants to see everyone using computers—but in his educational philosophy, like Suppes, he tends to conservatism. Suppes and Braun have a large following for their past work. Both favor materials that are self-contained and intended to teach the students largely independently of teachers present. Moreover, neither the teachers nor the students are required to learn anything about computers except how to turn them on and off.

The real educational impact of computers, as Dwyer and others, such as Albrecht and Ahl, see it, comes from personally using them—programming them. Bob Albrecht, whose readers know him as the Dragon, focuses on elementary education. He started a computer storefront, a drop-in center (in Menlo Park, California, in the early 1970s), in which computing power was made available to anyone dropping in. He also began publishing computer magazines for children, teachers, and hobbyists. He has helped to start several magazines, for example, *People's Computer Company* and its replacement, *Recreational Computing*; *Computers and Calculators*; and *Dr. Dobbs' Journal*. One of his BASIC manuals has been adopted for many of the popular microcomputers. Albrecht has written columns in his and other magazines. He has dedicated many years to trying to give people computing power in any form for personal purposes.

Another activist who has approached computers and education through magazine power and thus realized national distribution is David Ahl. Ahl, founder and editor-in-chief of *Creative Computing*, designed the magazine to appeal to the home computer and hobbyist audience. The magazine, which ceased publishing in December 1985, was large and wide ranging in levels of sophistication. *Creative Computing* was directed toward people looking for software, courseware, and gameware in print, on tape, on disk, etc. and for "off the shelf" computer hardware. Its goal was to infuse people with an enthusiasm and a sense of belonging to a movement—the personal computer movement—to something larger than themselves. Ahl himself has probably introduced more novices to computing than any other person in the country, as he has been a speaker or a workshop leader or an exhibitor at most personal computer shows around the country.

In the 1980s, a strong spokesperson for BASIC in schools has been Arthur Luehrmann, who had actively used BASIC in courses at Dartmouth. He has been a promoter of standardizing BASIC and of introducing structured BASIC. He left Dartmouth to become director of computing activities at the Lawrence Hall of Science at Berkeley, California, where he expanded this public access place to reach out to schools in the area. He then founded

Computer Literacy, a company that produces textbooks. Luehrmann suggests that BASIC be introduced in the school curriculum in the seventh grade. He has also developed material for Pascal. Luehrmann writes for popular computer magazines in support of programming as an important societal skill (Luehrmann 1980, 1983, 1984).

Thus Dwyer, Ahl, Albrecht, Luehrmann, and others in the BASIC culture have a more romantic and revolutionary vision of the computer's potential impact on the educational process than either Braun or Suppes do. For Dwyer and some of the others in the BASIC culture, BASIC was the language of choice because it was the language available. As Logo, Pascal, LISP, and other languages become available, their language of choice is in flux.

In what follows I offer some criticisms of BASIC as a language for learning and as a carrier of powerful computational ideas.

BASIC

BASIC was designed in the early 1960s by John Kemeny and Tom Kurtz. Kemeny saw the need at Los Alamos and other government projects for fast computing by scientists and engineers, extending the capabilities of slide rules in much the same way that programmable calculators do now. The commands or key words needed for this kind of activity were few. The intention was to maximize the communication between human and computer, man-machine symbiosis, by restricting what was asked of either of them. Arithmetic and trigonometric functions were needed. Stored programs were needed for repeated calculations and error detecting. A control structure for repeating parts of the program was needed (FOR loop). A way of using pieces of the program at certain times was needed (branching with GOTO). Some text manipulation (string handling) was added as a feature but the primary focus was on labeling and performing calculations. BASIC was designed for a specific audience to replace FORTRAN. The audience was to be calculus students, scientists, or engineers who needed to compute complex series of calculations repeatedly.

In the early 1960s Kemeny negotiated for Dartmouth a business agreement with General Electric, on whose computer the Dartmouth Time-Sharing System (DTSS) was built. The time-sharing system was designed around BASIC as the programming language. Digital Equipment Corporation and other computer companies began to offer BASIC on their computers. Kemeny and others at Dartmouth established BASIC groups such as Project COMPUTe and later CONDUIT now centered at the University of Iowa. The user community grew.

There are now committees to standardize BASIC. CONDUIT offers programs written in BASIC as annotated packages for university courses.

The Minnesota Educational Computing Consortium (MECC) offers "debugged" programs in BASIC for the Apple and other microcomputers for elementary and secondary school children and teachers. Computer stores sell different dialects of BASIC and programs written in them to consumers. I mention these business arrangements and organizational support mechanisms because they are part of what has helped institutionalize and spread BASIC and some of the considerations people use in joining the community of BASIC users. Nonetheless, BASIC was designed in reaction to batch-processing FORTRAN and was intended to be as efficient as possible in terms of computer considerations of space and time. Human time was cheap by comparison, and yet part of BASIC's cost effectiveness lay in its specificity and accessibility. It was targeted to be a powerful programmable slide rule.

BASIC is advertised as a language that has few primitives (commands or key words) and so can be learned quickly. Students can quickly learn to use it as a desk calculator. They could convert algorithms they already understand in their math or science courses to BASIC programs. But what of the people who do not understand the math and science algorithms? What of the people who want to use the computer for nonnumeric programming? In partial response to these questions and partially as a reflection of other views of how to harness the computer, people have been developing simulations in which there is less emphasis on the user becoming proficient at programming and more emphasis on developing convivial tools for the user to explore a particular problem domain—simulations of economic models in a more sophisticated way than, for example, the Huntington materials. For many microcomputer enthusiasts the way to build these environments is to have a cluster of computers networked to one another and to a central data base. Dwyer, for example, began to develop simulation environments that his students could explore. The students could also change and extend the scope of the simulation by using extended BASIC. Dwyer's Solo/NET/works Project endeavors to develop a multicomputer system to support "inventive learning" (Dwyer and Critchfield 1982).

Critiquing BASIC as a Carrier of Powerful Ideas

Microcomputers offer users more computing power than what most people had on large time-shared computers. Television sets are used for displaying conversations with the computer and also for displaying video games with moving pictures. Students want to write their own programs to make video games or display pictures. In a procedural language such as Logo, students can apply problem-solving techniques in the style of Polya—breaking problems into simpler components, doing what you know how to do, and so on. These pieces cannot be done procedurally in BASIC because BASIC is not a procedural language. The pieces cannot be debugged, named, and then forgotten until they are needed, as they can be in Logo, or procedurized, as they can be in Pascal and Logo. In BASIC, pieces of code are referred to by line number, and the flow of the program can be altered by conditional statements; but only one program can be in the work space at any given time, and adding new features to the language is not possible for a beginning programmer.

Dwyer wants novices to be able to use computers in sophisticated ways. Developing the necessary programming expertise to build a large simulation in BASIC, for example, might take too long. Thus Dwyer would like to move toward developing kits or environments that users interact with, extend, or use to build larger programs. Because it is not procedural, BASIC does not make building such kits for users easy.

There is another problem for classroom teachers that is causing many of them to look toward the development of materials. Teachers are finding BASIC difficult to use with their students. Sometimes the attitude is expressed by saying that perhaps, after all, programming is something most people will not be good at or like to do. Often this happens when teachers have not been given a chance to use the computer themselves in an exploratory fashion. Often it happens when teachers think of ways for thirty children to share one computer. Often it happens when teachers are asked to integrate the computer into their regular math classroom activities. Then children are asked to translate algorithms from their math texts to a computer language. The problem here is that if the child does not already know the algorithm, working on the computer does not help much. The computer is an incentive, but often with this kind of problem the child does not know if the program is doing its job.

One of the problems teachers have in teaching children to program is that they emphasize learning the vocabulary and grammar of a programming language instead of emphasizing the process of exploring ideas. For the most part, teachers are not experienced in introducing computational ideas to the children. They do not have in mind examples of programming activities or experience in helping children to pursue their own interests and in using the language to express their own ideas. These problems are more apparent in BASIC programming environments because BASIC is an algebraic, nonprocedural language; the language does not lend itself to thinking about building user tools in it. It does not allow users to add easily new key words to those already in the language.

Some difficulties in BASIC programming come from its algebraic nature and from the kinds of examples for which it is helpful, such as

MULT.TABLE. There are many directions that a programmer can take, but there is still the question of how a child becomes a solo programmer. These projects, whether they are written in BASIC or Logo, have a common flaw for beginning students: They are confined to translating algorithms into a typewriter environment. Dwyer responded to this problem in his laboratory by attaching devices to the computer for plotting or making music. Dwyer worked primarily with junior and senior high school students and college students within the context of doing algebra or physics; the deficiencies of the algebraic language BASIC pale in comparison with the alienated mathematics of classroom algebra without BASIC programming.

Thus in Dwyer's discussions there is a conflict between the heuristic procedures and strategies that exist in the head and the programs that are actually written in BASIC. This conflict is being felt within the BASIC community, and there have been several efforts to structure BASIC and make it procedural (Kemeny and Kurtz 1985). The dialects of BASIC popular on microcomputers and in use in schools and homes today are not procedural. The limitations of BASIC as a language for learning about powerful ideas in computer science are being felt. In colleges and universities Pascal, which is a procedural language, is becoming popular. Some believe that the way around the problem is to create more laboratory materials—games, quizzes, drills, etc. Others, like Seymour Papert and Alan Kay, believe that a powerful language for learning should be developed in which children can then grow.

The creators of BASIC, Kemeny and Kurtz, have become vocal critics of BASIC as it has evolved on microcomputers. At Dartmouth during the 1970s BASIC underwent several transformations. But it is the early version of BASIC that was used as a model for microcomputers. Kemeny and Kurtz criticize these implementations for "tiny computers, so that severe compromises had to be made":

Some of these compromises were ugly and violated our design principles for the language. But people got used to them, and many programs were written in these poor versions of BASIC. (Kemeny and Kurtz 1985, p. 55)

Furthermore, they contend that different implementations take advantage of the special hardware features of different computers so that "no two of these implementations are compatible." The authors go on to say that they "are concerned that a generation of students is growing up learning Street BASIC":

An apt description, we believe. Vernacular street talk varies from location to location and year to year, and is full of vulgarisms not to be used in polite surroundings.

Unfortunately, the same is true for BASIC. (Kemeny and Kurtz 1985, p.56)

They also feel "that this is directly relevant to the problem that whereas schools now have hardware, educational software lags far behind."

There have been devastating criticisms of BASIC in the literature. Unfortunately, as it applies to Street BASIC, we agree with them. (Kemeny and Kurtz 1985, p. 56)

The strongly expressed disapproval of microcomputer dialects of BASIC by its creators has come at a time when they have prepared their Structured BASIC for microcomputers; it is called True BASIC. Programmers, implementers of software written in microcomputer dialects of BASIC, dismiss these criticisms. The education community cannot. Street BASIC is becoming the language taught in junior high; it is sandwiched between Logo, which is taught in elementary school, and Pascal, which is taught in high school.

Talking about Dartmouth's BASIC in the early 1970s, Kemeny and Kurtz say:

As we entered the decade of the seventies, there was scant warning about the computing revoluations brewing. We had settled back to enjoy our new version of BASIC the Sixth. Little did we realize the impact that fancy graphics and structured programming would have by the end of the decade. And there was little hint that within a dozen years we would have computers sitting on our desktops that would be as powerful as the huge central time-sharing system that served us so well. (Kemeny and Kurtz 1985, p. 39)

This statement seems a bit ludicrous in light of the Logo work going on in Cambridge, Massachusetts, in the late 1960s and early 1970s.

Conflicts in Conveying Powerful Ideas

In this section I discuss a particular programming project (Dwyer 1977b; Dwyer and Critchfield 1978; Critchfield 1979). The program raises important issues about the effects of BASIC programming on good programming style and on making use of powerful ideas from computer science.

The program consists of five nested FOR loops. The suggestion is made that this problem "is also related to the important idea of *tree structures*" (Dwyer and Critchfield 1978, p.60. Here is the statement of the problem:

THE HOT DOG PROBLEM

Suppose you're running the hotdog stand at your next club picnic, and you decide to post a computer printout showing how to order all the possible combinations by number. Let's assume that there are only YES/NO decisions allowed for hot dog, bun, mustard, mayonnaise, and catsup. To discourage overindulgence, we'll also print a calorie count for each combination.

The way to think about this problem is to picture what's called a *decision tree*.

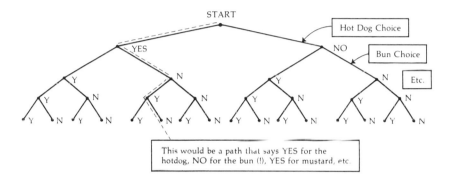

One way to generate a tree structure in BASIC is to use nested FOR loops, one for each level. Our tree will have five levels (one for each ingredient) so there will be five FOR loops. Here's how all the paths through our five-level tree can be tabulated with a BASIC program.

LIST

```
10  PRINT "        DOG   BUN   MUST.  MAYO.  CATSUP"
15  LET X=1
20  FOR H = 0 TO 1
30  FOR B = 0 TO 1
40  FOR M = 0 TO 1
50  FOR Y = 0 TO 1
60  FOR C = 0 TO 1
70  PRINT"#";K;":   ";
80  PRINT H;"     ";B;"     ";M;"     ";Y;"     ";C;
90  PRINT " CALORIES=";H*140+B*120+M*20+Y*100+C*30
95  LET K=K+1
100 NEXT C
110 NEXT Y
120 NEXT M
```

```
130 NEXT B
140 NEXT H
150 END

RUN
```

	DOG	BUN	MUST.	MAYO.	CATSUP	
# 1 :	0	0	0	0	0	CALORIES= 0
# 2 :	0	0	0	0	1	CALORIES= 30
# 3 :	0	0	0	1	0	CALORIES= 100
# 4 :	0	0	0	1	1	CALORIES= 130
# 5 :	0	0	1	0	0	CALORIES= 20
# 6 :	0	0	1	0	1	CALORIES= 50
# 7 :	0	0	1	1	0	CALORIES= 120
# 8 :	0	0	1	1	1	CALORIES= 150
# 9 :	0	1	0	0	0	CALORIES= 120
# 10 :	0	1	0	0	1	CALORIES= 150
# 11 :	0	1	0	1	0	CALORIES= 220
# 12 :	0	1	0	1	1	CALORIES= 250
# 13 :	0	1	1	0	0	CALORIES= 140
# 14 :	0	1	1	0	1	CALORIES= 170
# 15 :	0	1	1	1	0	CALORIES= 240
# 16 :	0	1	1	1	1	CALORIES= 270
# 17 :	1	0	0	0	0	CALORIES= 140
# 18 :	1	0	0	0	1	CALORIES= 170
# 19 :	1	0	0	1	0	CALORIES= 240
# 20 :	1	0	0	1	1	CALORIES= 270
# 21 :	1	0	1	0	0	CALORIES= 160
# 22 :	1	0	1	0	1	CALORIES= 190
# 23 :	1	0	1	1	0	CALORIES= 260
# 24 :	1	0	1	1	1	CALORIES= 290
# 25 :	1	1	0	0	0	CALORIES= 260
# 26 :	1	1	0	0	1	CALORIES= 290
# 27 :	1	1	0	1	0	CALORIES= 360
# 28 :	1	1	0	1	1	CALORIES= 390
# 29 :	1	1	1	0	0	CALORIES= 280
# 30 :	1	1	1	0	1	CALORIES= 310
# 31 :	1	1	1	1	0	CALORIES= 380
# 32 :	1	1	1	1	1	CALORIES= 410

(Dwyer and Critchfield 1978, p. 61)

This program, as an example of a decision tree, is misleading. One reason for using a tree structure is to take advantage of its dynamic nature. The user might not know or care initially about the size of the structure, that is, whether there are two levels or five levels. What the user cares about is the relationship among the data and a description of how you get from one path or node of the tree to another.

In this problem, the choices are independent of one another. Prior decisions do not influence the current decisions. For example, all the nodes at level 2 represent decisions about buns, and level 3 nodes represent mustard, regardless of whether a bun was chosen or not. The paths are constrained.

There is an additional sense of artificiality to the problem: The program depends on the fact that this binary tree is balanced. That is, its left side or branch is the same as its right branch. But one of the powerful ideas behind tree structures are that they do not have to be balanced. The programmer can abstractly describe how to traverse a tree knowing only that it is a binary tree.

The general characteristic of trees is that they are hierarchical representations of data. There is a logical ordering to the information contained in the tree. Thus it matters *when* the program makes a choice, unlike the problem posed here. It really does not matter which item is chosen first or second, etc. There is an assumption that the ordering of hot dog, bun, mustard, mayo, and catsup is important to the problem, but the outcome is the same. All possible combinations will be printed. This leads to a further confusion when the "decision tree" idea is introduced. A decision tree is used to help find optimal paths, but here we are not told to do that.

In this well-intentioned attempt to relate the BASIC control structure of FOR loops to tree structures, several issues are raised about the relationship between programming and ideas from computer science to enhance problem solving. FOR loops cannot "generate a tree structure." They can simulate certain results. Following paths in a tree requires two actions—going down a branch from a node and going back up the branch to the node (backtracking) so that a new branch of the tree can be followed. FOR loops are unidirectional; the flow of the program can go up or down but not both.

The essentially recursive nature of trees is also ignored. By definition, a tree is composed of other trees or subtrees. Thus the program should be able to operate from anywhere in the tree, but doing this requires backtracking, and FOR loops do not allow that. This program always starts at the topmost or root node and then follows a path to its terminal node. Thus, although the program prints out thirty-two paths and their respective calorie counts and although these paths could be traced out on a tree, there is no mathematical connection between the program and the ideas it is meant to represent. These are two parallel but different processes. The program never backtracks. In other words the program goes outside of the intended data representation; it does not trace a path and then retrace as it generates new branches but instead computes thirty-two separate routes one at a time.

Although the program does not make use of tree structures, Dwyer does. In his mind he solves the problem using a binary tree. For Dwyer, a computer scientist, procedural thinking is part of his "heuristic strategies." In Dwyer's mind and in his planning with pencil and paper, procedures are definite entities, but in BASIC they do not exist.

In programming cultures like those of LISP, Pascal, and Logo, in which procedures and hierarchical structures have been given concrete identity, programmers find powerful metaphors in tree searches and in recursive processes. There is a tendency to anthropomorphize, to look at control mechanisms among procedures and within the flow of procedures in terms of actors or demons, or other creatures resident in the computer capable of giving advice, passing data, receiving data, activating procedures, changing procedures, etc. As we will see in chapter 5, this is a phenomenon of the Logo computer culture, and it is common to other computer cultures in which recursive and procedural thinking is embedded in the language. It is this aspect that Davis finds so attractive and useful in applying to mathematical behavior. In the Logo culture the intention is to share these and other powerful ideas with children as they develop.

Programming style covers a large area, but the one of most concern here is not readability of code but extensibility and clarity of thought, that is, whether or not the programmer can build on what he or she has done. This might take the form of adapting a program to other purposes or extending the programming idea to enhance everyday problem-solving activities. One idea that comes immediately to mind is giving objects names so that they can be referred to easily; this extends itself to using programs to create other programs, to being able to think of a program as a piece of a job, a sub-process, etc. Another idea involves communicating between programs, passing data—again something that is possible to do in procedural languages. Another powerful idea having to do with organizing thoughts is thinking of different kinds of information structures—data structures such as simple lists, arrays, stacks, queues, list structure of different kinds, tree structures, and even the programs themselves.

Procedural languages such as Pascal and Logo give programmers an opportunity to think about these structures and to create their own and use them. BASIC, on the other hand, is not procedural and does not have list structures; its objects are organized linearly as simple lists or strings or in multidimensional arrays. But clever programming can often bring about the same effect as a program written in Logo or Pascal. The previous discussion of a BASIC programming project shows some of the difficulties that a restricted programming language can create and that good programmers almost automatically compensate for; that is, they find ways to code around or reconfigure the problem.

Eclecticism

The eclectic nature of the BASIC culture is reflected in the belief that computers can be anyone's tool for any number of purposes. This can be achieved by adding appropriate gadgetry (hardware to the computer so that it can be extended to music, art, physics, etc. and by debugging programs by either removing bugs or coding around them. There seems to be a gap that this eclecticism does not resolve. How do we introduce children and other novices to this learning environment? What theoretical framework can we operate from? That is, as teachers, what insights into children's acquisition of knowledge does this learning environment offer?)

Dwyer's teaching strategies are deeply tied to one principle: respect for the individual. This principle is supported in different ways. For example, in dual mode learning the teacher respects the uniqueness of the individual and does not try to impose his or her own way of doing things because it does not help the learner; instead the teacher helps the student develop his or her own method.

This process can be approached in three different ways that ideally are intertwined. The three approaches are transmittal, experiential, and creative. Transmittal techniques, like those used by Suppes, are totally unacceptable by themselves, according to Dwyer. As one kind of technique at the disposal of the student and thus in the student's control, it is often useful; but learning takes place experientially. Thus the teacher helps by extending the learning environment into different domains, often by adding new "gadgets." Writing programs and using them are all part of experiential learning. Creative mode sets in through debugging programs, understanding why they do not work, and then fixing them so that they do work.

For most people, inventive solo learning requires both a supportive social environment, and a supportive physical environment. This means the right kind of guidance, instruction, encouragement, criticism, written materials, time, space, and equipment. (Dwyer and Critchfield 1982, p. 8)

Dwyer concentrates in his discussions on learning on the process of teaching. Dwyer sees the mind as a black box and therefore as something that cannot really be discussed. He has absorbed the ideas of Newell and Simon, Minsky and Papert and others whose theoretical work on thinking has led to new insights into the mind and thus to how knowledge is represented and how it is acquired. Dwyer believes that there are internal mental structures that are built up by the individual in some way. Teachers using these three different approaches help the students to build their own internal models. Dwyer does not go further.

On this point he differs from Papert and in this difference lies the key distinction between their learning environments. Dwyer's is built on techniques and gadgets and adapting tools to education, thus following in an eclectic tradition. Papert's environment is embedded in a theoretical foundation that has its roots in the study of thinking and which molds a computer environment into an instrument for children to use in their intellectual development.

Some Concluding Remarks

I agree with the spirit of what Dwyer says and much of what he envisions, but I have been arguing that his work is blighted by a *basic* inconsistency. There is an inconsistency in Dwyer's vision between the environment he wants and the tools with which he chooses to construct this environment. He uses tools created for other purposes than the one at hand, but he chooses them because they are "on the shelf," and so he does not heed his own advice: "Although I would be the last to advocate designing educational systems by engineering-like formulae, it seems to me that attempting to innovate with supportive systems that don't begin to match the sophistication of the human learner should be viewed as a betrayal, not a consequence, of a humanistic approach to education" (Dwyer 1971a, p. 100).

For example, in programming he adopts the BASIC language because it is easily available. The significance of this comes from the limited degree of control over the computational medium given by BASIC. In fact, for most children BASIC is so inaccessible that *no* control is given. BASIC is a primitive programming language that challenges expert programmers to "code around" its limitations. Of course, there is a sense of personal accomplishment when the programmer breaks through these limitations, but the point is that the language that might be easy to *learn* is *hard* to *use* and shuts out aspects of this environment for many people, including elementary school children.

Similarly in the arts Dwyer's colleague Critchfield writes about "computer experience in the manner of artistic creation" (Critchfield 1979, p. 18). The tools given to the student in this computer experience are a color TV connected to the computer with a light-sensitive pen by which the computer can light up a screen position when the pen points to it. The student uses the pen in conjunction with a program that places points on the screen and then draws lines from those points to ones chosen by the student. The student can select different colors for each of the lines. Thus the student can draw ellipses, circles, sine waves, straight lines, etc. "There are endless possibilities" (Critchfield 1979, p. 21). An alternative to the student is to write his or her own programs using the BASIC commands PLOT or POKE, thus lighting up individual points on the screen.

There is a clear conflict here between intention and the tools at hand. Is this a genuine artistic experience? What kind of art can students achieve with a small microcomputer? Even the art obtained with the best computers is limited. Even at the leading edge of computer technology applied to art, the products are, at best, just beginning to qualify as art. Thus Nicholas Negroponte, a leading figure in aesthetic uses of the computer, a professor of architecture, and a specialist in computer graphics has spoken rather critically of work in computers and art.

Rarely have two disciplines joined forces seemingly to bring out the worst in each other as have computers and art. A mixture of mathematical exercises has predominated in the search for ways to use computers in general and computer graphics in particular for the purpose of achieving a new art form, or simply art, or both. The symmetry and periodicity of the Lissajous figures (easily generated curves on TV screens), transformations into and out of recognizable patterns, and the happenstance of stochastic processing epitomize the current palette of gadgetry used by either the playful computer scientist or the inquiring artist in the name of art. While their intentions may be good, the results are predominantly bad art and petty programming. (Negroponte 1979, p. 21)

Negroponte's position is, perhaps, extreme; in the 1980s we have begun to see a significant improvement in the quality of computer-generated pictures. The computer graphics used in making films and video are becoming powerful artistic tools. But one thing is certain: In order to produce any approximation to a genuine artistic experience, more was needed than could be provided by a microcomputer experience of the sort "on the shelf" before 1983, when Apple introduced its Macintosh. Macintosh offered users an opportunity to use a painting program similar to the ones built by Alan Kay and his colleagues at the Xerox Palo Alto Research Center in the 1970s. The paint program on the Macintosh does not have color, but it allows the user to mix gray-scaled patterns in a variety of ways.

This discussion points to something else, and that is computer graphics is a multidimensional medium that is visually attractive and intellectually compelling. It has led to the spread of a new mathematics, one based on the computer, of which Papert's turtle geometry is one example (discussed in chapter 5).

Nonetheless, the gap between the realization of personalizing the computer's power and the tools offered by which to do it is not easily closed in the BASIC computer environment. Often the programmer becomes inured to the difficulties and more enthusiastic over small victories than warranted, thus building bridges that can be seen only by the programmer, not by other people in the environment.

5

Papert: Constructivism and Piagetian Learning

Although Suppes, Davis, and Dwyer propose three different computer-based learning environments, they seem to share a common view of the content of school mathematics: that it consist of arithmetic, algebra, and geometry and that it be teachable. Papert has a different view of the content of present-day mathematics. He sees most of present-day school mathematics as denatured and alienating and outside of a child's concerns. He sees the computer as a way to create new learning conditions and new things to learn. He envisions the computer as a "mathland," in which the computer becomes an instrument for children to talk in mathematics about their everyday life experiences and in which children learn mathematics as naturally as they learn to speak. Papert designed Logo as a language for learning. He developed the turtle, a mathematical entity, with which children could identify and develop a personal relationship.

Papert defines mathematics in its broadest sense. Mathematics is a source of powerful ideas resulting in rigorous, logical thinking with applications to all activities—to the whole person and to the whole environment. Mathematics is not a collection of facts or techniques, although facts and techniques are by-products. Mathematics provides ideas that help people to think about their lives, organize knowledge, and develop socially, emotionally, and intellectually. This "holistic" view of mathematics is supported by the computer's presence.

Papert sees learning as a constructive process. He believes that one of Piaget's most important contributions is not that there are stages of development but that people possess different theories about the world. Children's theories contrast sharply with adult theories. Piaget showed that even babies have theories, which are modified as the children grow. For Papert, the process by which these theories are transformed is a constructivist one. Children build their own intellectual structures. They use readily available materials, which they find in their own cultures. Papert pursues such questions as, What experiences and knowledge lead children to change their theories, and why do they learn some things without formal instruction and not learn other things despite formal instruction? These and other such questions motivate Papert's research.

Papert believes that children learn best when then are encouraged to draw on their own intuition and put to use what they already know in developing new ideas. He sees the computer as providing a context in which this kind of learning can happen. For this to happen, the computer's assets have to be molded to the children's needs and a new kind of mathematics that coincides with natural developmental learning processes has to be invented.

Papert has been actively engaged in pursuing this goal. His vision of computers emerges as many images each linked to one another. Underlying his vision is a goal of creating conditions for people and computers to form relationships with one another that will enhance both people's sense of themselves as learners and their self worth.

The kind of mathematics Papert has in mind for elementary school children is thus constructive and intuitive rather than rule driven and formal. This mathematics builds on unique characteristics of computer technology and science. One example is turtle geometry. Papert's geometry differs as radically as most modern geometries differ from present school practice. It is a modern mathematics that could not exist before computers. It is a computational geometry, but it differs in other ways from plane or analytic geometry. It is an investigation into object construction; using descriptive methods it draws on personal experiences and personal interactions with the objects. Its descriptive power is dynamic and process oriented. It draws on informal methods and heuristics based on personal knowledge. Mathematical ideas, instead of being encountered formally, are first introduced as entities, such as people, with their own peculiarities. This approach to mathematics follows within a tradition of intuitionism and constructivism shared by many other mathematicians, including Poincaré, Brouwer, and Gödel (Papert 1978c; Hofstadter 1979).

Mathematical ideas, like programs and even computers themselves, are thought of as living things that can be constructed (described) and that can take on different characteristics. This anthropomorphic approach has been a powerful heuristic tool in scientific thought (for example, Maxwell's demon, Poincaré's sentinel, Freud's id. In this computational world it is used often. The users can talk about what programs do and what they want them to do. They can also talk about bugs and their features.

Turtle Geometry

To appreciate the methodological aspects of the constructivist approach, a technical discussion of some aspects of Papert's computational geometry is needed. The mathematical entity in this geometric world is known as a turtle. Its name is derived from Grey Walter's cybernetic invention, the tortoise. The first turtle existed in the physical world, looking very much like a big yellow cannister-type vacuum cleaner on large wheels with a pen in the middle of its belly; this was in 1970. The floor turtle was followed quickly by a graphics turtle, which lives on a TV screen. Turtles crawl around leaving a trace of their path, or not, as the programmer wishes. They can be used to construct objects. These objects can then be used to create new objects. Object construction is thus given tangible expression. The graphics turtle is not only an instrument for drawing geometric objects; it can also be directed to create animated sequences made up of its individual drawings. In some implementations of Logo and turtle graphics, several turtles can exist at the same time.[1]

Constructing a Turtle Circle

Imagine, for the moment, that you are in Papert's computer-based learning environment, his mathland. One of its computational entities is a turtle (figure 5.1). This particular turtle lives on a TV screen. The turtle can travel about the screen and mark its path because it has a pen. The turtle moves in the direction or away from the direction it faces. The turtle can be commanded to move FORWARD (or BACK) a number of steps or to pivot LEFT (or RIGHT) a number of degrees. Now, in trying to understand turtle behavior, it is possible for you, the programmer (child or adult, novice or expert), to stand up and obey these commands as if you were the turtle. So, if you want to make turtle circles on the screen, a natural first step would be to walk in a circle and observe your own behavior. (It is often helpful to observe someone else.) By standing up and tracing out a path of a circle your first observation might be, "I walk in a curve." That is true; that is what a circle is. Now how are you doing that? What actions do you take that make you walk in a curve? "I go forward a little bit of a step and turn a little bit at the same time." Now you try that idea on the turtle:

```
FORWARD 1
RIGHT 1
```

The turtle obeys, and you see a small movement. In Logo you can put those commands into a procedure that you can run repeatedly:

```
TO CIRCLEBIT
FORWARD 1
RIGHT 1
END
```

You do not need to know to begin with how many times to run this process. You can just try a number of times. So

```
REPEAT 100 [CIRCLEBIT]
```

(figure 5.2). Not enough. So

```
REPEAT 300 [CIRCLEBIT]
```

(figure 5.3). It did it! Now you can put the whole process in a procedure. This time, I use 360, the number of degrees in a circle, as the number of times to repeat

```
TO CIRCLE
REPEAT 360 [CIRCLEBIT]
END
```

You have a circle procedure. You can construct a circle. The turtle walks in a circle following that description and you can, too. The relationship between the computational description and what a circle is and how a circle is made (a closed figure of constant curvature) becomes readily apparent. The relationship between what you do in walking in a circle and the computational description are also close to one another. After all, you used your own body movement to plan it out. Thus this mathematics is intuitive and personal and understandable by young children.

This contrasts sharply with the usual way circles are thought about in school, where we are presented with either

$C = 2 * \pi * R$ Plane Geometry

or

$X^2 + Y^2 = R^2$ Cartesian Geometry

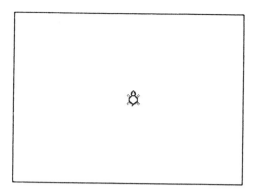

Figure 5.1
A graphics turtle .

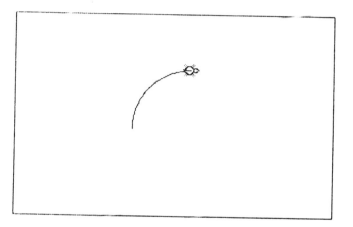

Figure 5.2
Position of turtle after the instruction REPEAT 100 [CIRCLEBIT].

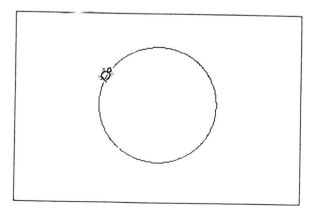

Figure 5.3
Position of turtle after the instruction REPEAT 300 [CIRCLEBIT]

as equations *about* circles. In the plane geometry equation, π is the ratio between a circle's circumference and its diameter, and we know π = 3.14159..., or 22/7. So, if we know the diameter we can compute the circumference, and vice versa. The Cartesian equation describes the relationship of each point along the circumference of a circle of radius *R* to the circle's center point. But neither of these equations *describes* a circle, that is, what a circle looks like. They tell us how to test for circularity but not what a circle *is*. We cannot intuitively derive these equations from thinking about circles. Nor can we derive circles from thinking about these equations.

The turtle example, on the other hand, gives us a foundation for understanding these equations and even for using them. We could use Descartes's equation to generate points along the circumference. We could use the plane geometry equation as well. For example, we could use it to change the CIRCLE procedure so that circles of different sizes (diameters) could be drawn.

As it happens these equations are useful to us in the real world of microcomputer graphics, where we have to trade off between precision and flexibility for everyday tools used for many purposes. Instead of a 360-side figure representing a circle (already a compromise, perhaps), we settle for a 20-side figure. This will do because the graphics screen is "coarser" than our ideal world and has about 100*100 positions on the screen. So instead of turning 1 degree on each round (bit) of the process, the turtle will turn 18 degrees or 360/20, that is, the total curvature divided by the number of sides. Now we compute the FORWARD step based on the plane geometry equation scaled to the number of sides in the figure (twenty is what we chose). Thus

```
TO CIRCLE :DIAMETER
REPEAT 360 [CIRCLEBIT :DIAMETER]
END


TO CIRCLEBIT :DIAMETER
FORWARD 22/7.*:DIAMETER/20
RIGHT 18
END
```

A Cartesian Circle

The contrast between turtle geometry and other approaches is captured in the advertisement (figure 5.4) for Pascal as opposed to BASIC. Although the intention of this ad was to show off Pascal's features over BASIC's, the point seems to get lost because of the choice of algorithm for drawing a circle. This advertisement is appropriate as an endorsement of turtle geometry. UCSD-Pascal, a popular version of Pascal running on microcomputers such as the Apple II, includes turtle geometry commands. The programs use Descartes's method to compute X and Y using trigonometric functions to compute the new X and Y positions.

Our turtle knows about Cartesian coordinates, and so the commands MOVE and DRAW are equivalent to the following Logo procedures:

```
TO MOVE :X :Y    TO DRAW :X :Y
PENUP            PENDOWN
SETXY :X :Y      SETXY :X :Y
END              END
```

But using these commands gives us no clue as to how to move ourselves. They ignore the direction in which the turtle is facing and just send it to a position on the screen. The turtle commands tell us to go forward in the direction we are facing and turn a little bit (to the right or the left). We ourselves can carry out those actions as if we were the turtle. We can use our body movement to figure out how to make a circle; we can draw a circle by following our own intuitive behavior. In the other case, as with school mathematics, we are dependent on knowing a position on the grid (graph) and computing the next position in terms of Cartesian coordinates using a formula, not our intuition and our body.

The program draws the circle in a counterclockwise direction. The process is not emphasized; it is as if counterclockwise is the direction circles are drawn. (In a fixed interpretation of coordinate geometry this notion becomes so.) Turtle geometry is much more personal. The turtle, like ourselves, can draw circles either by turning left or by turning right; the decision is in the hands of the programmer.

The turtle sits on the circumference and needs only to go forward and to turn alternately in small steps. Big steps have a dramatic effect. If we change the input to both FORWARD and RIGHT, for example,

REPEAT 360 [FORWARD 90 RIGHT 90],

then the turtle draws ninety squares, one on top of the other.

REPEAT 360 [FORWARD 90 RIGHT 156]

results in a 30-point star (figure 5.5).

What's the difference between BASIC and Pascal?

COMPARE THESE APPROACHES TO DRAWING A CIRCLE

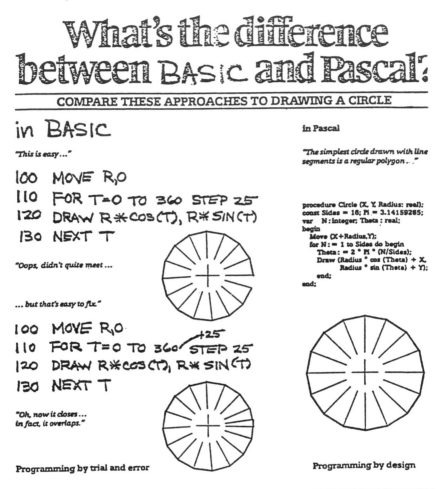

in BASIC

"This is easy..."

```
100   MOVE R,O
110   FOR T=0 TO 360 STEP 25
120   DRAW R*COS(T), R*SIN(T)
130   NEXT T
```

"Oops, didn't quite meet ...

... but that's easy to fix."

```
100   MOVE R,O
110   FOR T=0 TO 360  +25
                   STEP 25
120   DRAW R*COS(T), R* SIN(T)
130   NEXT T
```

*"Oh, now it closes...
in fact, it overlaps."*

Programming by trial and error

in Pascal

*"The simplest circle drawn with line
segments is a regular polygon..."*

```
procedure Circle (X, Y, Radius: real);
const Sides = 16; PI = 3.14159285;
var   N : integer; Theta : real;
begin
    Move (X+Radius,Y);
    for N := 1 to Sides do begin
        Theta: = 2 ° PI ° (N/Sides);
        Draw (Radius ° cos (Theta) + X,
              Radius ° sin (Theta) + Y);
        end;
end;
```

Programming by design

GET IT RIGHT THE FIRST TIME

Figure 5.4
Advertisement promoting Pascal over BASIC.

Figure 5.5
A 30-point star made from the command REPEAT 360 [FORWARD 90 RIGHT 156].

Piaget and Mathematics

Piaget's research provided Papert with a large body of successful examples describing children's learning without explicit teaching and curricula. Papert sees Piaget as "the theorist of what children can learn by themselves without the intervention of educators" (Papert 1980d, p. 994). Piaget, for example, studied children acquiring conservation of number. Their discoveries about number are demonstrated by asking children of different ages questions about number. At some point, say four years old, the child gives incorrect answers to questions about number, and yet a few years later the same child "gets the 'adult' answer." "In Piaget's language the child will have acquired (I would say discovered) the conservation of number" (Papert 1980d, p. 994)

It is one thing to say that learning should continue in the same natural way it begins from birth; but to do so, conditions for this to happen must be created. Papert is a constructivist; he is neither an innatist (like Chomsky) nor an empiricist (like Suppes). His constructivism builds on Piaget's genetic epistemology model. For Papert, Piaget is

the theorist of children as the builders of their own intellectual structures. But they need materials to build with and the culture is their source. When the culture is rich in relevant materials they build well, stably and early. When the culture is poor in materials the building is impeded.

All present day cultures are rich in materials relevant to the construction of the kind of knowledge that underlies conservation of number. Most are particularly rich in examples of 1–1 correspondence, mother-father, shoe-foot, foot-foot and the many other things that come in pairs. I see all this as "material" for the notion of number. (Papert 1980d, p. 995)

But mathematics involves more than the notion of number. It is about understanding processes and computation, it is about understanding mechanisms of thought, and it is also about actively solving real problems, etc.:

But the present day cultures are poor in everything to do with procedure and process and in many other things related to computation such as all the aspects of self-reference and Gödel coding so beautifully discussed in *Gödel, Escher, Bach* by Douglas Hofstadter. Children build slowly, shakily or not at all where the natural form of the intellectual structure would use these "materials." Thus a common element of all hitherto existing cultures gives rise to a developmental universal. But the idea that there could be a computational culture shows that the "universal" is an artifact of history and not of human nature. (Papert 1980d, p. 995)

And so Papert sees the computer presence as a potential agent for changing not only how we do things but also how we grow up *thinking about* doing things.

Papert sees every thinking person as mathematically minded, but most people lose touch with their own mathematical mindedness. This estrangement Papert sees coming from the culture both in and out of school. He sees the culture supporting some mathematical ideas, such as the concept of number, but other powerful mathematical ideas, such as procedure and process and computation—dynamic instruments of thought—are not well represented in our culture as it is now. But with the computer presence there is ample evidence that significant changes could occur, and Papert's math-land examples might then be incorporated into our popular thinking.

Papert sees school mathematics as "denatured mathematics," as devital-ized mathematics, as depersonalized mathematics, because it is detached from things children think about, care about, and relate to. Papert stands firmly in the mathematical tradition of creative thinkers, for whom math-ematics and intellectual thought are personal, live, active, and interactive, as part of the process of making original contributions. Their sense of poetics, aesthetics, and beauty are based on a culture that is rich in personal metaphors and recognition of unique and different ways of looking at problems. Mathematical thought relates the individual to herself and to her world and helps to account for similarities and differences within people and within cultures. The unifying principle does not come from some logical system but from people's relationships, as interpreters and builders of their intellectual structures. This view of the relationship between mathematics and culture resonates with the ideas and attitudes expressed by others, in-cluding Davis and Dwyer.

Suppes, Davis, Dwyer, and Papert

In comparing Suppes, Davis, and Dwyer, differences among the three emerge; these differences are primarily related to their own experiences and are evident in their methods of instruction and their theories of how learning takes place. They seem to share a common view of the content of elementary mathematics:

math = (arithmetic + algebra + geometry).

They differ on when to introduce certain topics and on what ideas to emphasize, but they agree that children should learn a certain body of mathematics.

Seymour Papert raises a new issue for the educator. He proposes *new* content. In fact, he proposes to *invent* new mathematical topics. Coming to understand what he is setting out to do requires situating his ideas, as well as Suppes's, Davis's, and Dwyer's, into a philosophical perspective within the history of mathematics. In so doing, we come to grips with what the new math movement is about. In this case, Suppes and Davis captured the dichotomous nature of the new math movement of the 1960s. On the one hand, there are those who, like Suppes, introduced new content into the curriculum. They chose as the new content logic and set theory, which for them serve as the foundation of all mathematics. These ideas are part of a tradition in which the best known and most monumental work is Whitehead and Russell's *Principia Mathematica (PM)*, in which all of mathematics is reduced to logic. The consequence of this work has been enormous; it helped to create a new area of mathematics, mathematical logic, as separate from logic, an area of philosophy. It helped to revitalize another area of mathematics: the foundations of mathematics, an area of mathematics in which working mathematicians whether geometers, topologists, algebraists, or logicians return to now and again but which has been since *PM* dominated by those who support formal logical thinking as the foundation of mathematical thinking.

We see in Suppes's curriculum the influence of the *PM* point of view. Suppes dissects mathematics into component skills. His underlying philosophy supports the same old methods of teaching, in which the teacher gives knowledge to the children in discrete components. The difference is that now the teachers and children are supplied with a well-organized curriculum that reduces elementary mathematics to a hierarchy of discrete concepts.

Seymour Papert breaks radically with this reductionist view of reform in mathematics education, as do Davis and Dwyer. In Davis's curriculum we see an emphasis on the *process* of doing mathematics. He breaks from the *PM* tradition of approaching mathematics formally and of emphasizing formulas; he attempts to emphasize the intuitionist, constructivist tradition of working mathematicians doing their job. He seeks to develop in children heuristic strategies of mathematicians as they seek to make *use* of what they already know in solving new problems. But Davis maintains a classical view of how to become mathematically sophisticated. Papert, on the other hand, sees a need for a new content that emphasizes computational processes rather than arithmetic skills. The purpose of Papert's new content is to give children an intellectual environment in which they can discover and construct new ideas and learn from their own personal experiences in a content-rich and meaningful environment.

It is this tradition of the usefulness of mathematics on a personal rather than on an abstract level that Papert shares with Davis. A theorem for them has its importance not so much in its proof but in its usefulness as an instrument for making new mathematical constructions (or discoveries). Papert does not think that arithmetic is a rich area for child-originated discoveries.

Although Papert shares with Davis and Dwyer an emphasis on both ex-periential learning involving the *whole* child and children discovering math-ematical ideas for themselves, he departs radically from them on how this can happen. It is not enough to change the methods of teaching. His theory of how learning occurs, through children making constructions, which Davis supports, requires that the content children first encounter in school math-ematics be changed to accommodate their natural tendencies. He sees the mathematics of both Suppes and Davis as "denatured" mathematics. For Suppes, following in the tradition of Whitehead and Russell, this is all to the good; it is as it should be. For Davis, following in the intuitive and constructivist tradition, this would be a clear distortion of his intentions.

In a sense, Papert absorbs the intentions of both Suppes and Davis to change, on the one hand, the content of elementary mathematics, bringing it into line with modern ideas about the foundations of mathematics, and, on the other hand, the process of doing elementary school mathematics so that it draws on children's intuition and everyday commonsense thinking.

How Papert differs from Suppes, Davis, and Dwyer might be summed up in what I call the Papert principle: If you want to teach arithmetic to children, arithmetic might not be the best route into these ideas for an easy understanding of the topic. What is needed is a way of *mathematizing* the child; thereafter particular mathematical topics become easy.

Arithmetic consists of formal rules and algorithms that are not easy for most people to relate to or make discoveries with. What they need first are some experiences in which they can develop a mathematical way of think-ing. Of course, for Suppes and others in the tradition of the *PM*, logic represents mathematical thinking. Papert and others outside of the *PM* tradi-tion, in which logical thinking is presumed to be fundamental, see a mathematical way of thinking emerging from intuitive and constructivist activities from a "genetic theory of mathematics" (Papert 1978b, p. 113). Thus they seek to create a more personal content in which to learn mathematics. For Papert, learning is an active process of doing and thinking about what you do. This contrasts with the *PM* rule-driven approach, in which you learn through being told rules and through drill and practice in order to master certain prescribed basic skills.

Reductionism versus Constructivism

Perhaps a little more perspective on these two points of view which for our purposes are captured by those in the *PM* tradition and those outside of it, will sharpen this intellectual conflict. Throughout *PM*, Whitehead and Russell aimed at showing by logical argument that logic stands at the foundations of mathematics. They strove to present a unified explanation of nature through their logical vision of the fundamental principles underlying mathematics. All of nature would be subject to this system of rules. This reductionist presentation embodied in Whitehead and Russell's gigantic work came at a time when mathematics and other sciences were seeing a rich outpouring of discoveries, all leading away from such a reductionist theory. Reductionism paved the way for logic to become a powerful tool in the construction of new theoretical frameworks—a point that stands in contradistinction to logic and set theory as the foundation of mathematics. Notions that had been taken as universal and intuitive were being replaced by new ideas that at first seemed counterintuitive. There were many geometries and geometries of many spaces. Einstein and the theory of relativity were bursting on the intellectual scene.

The idea that there are many mathematical systems, each governed by different sets of rules, was becoming the unifying principle of modern science. In the face of this reality came *PM*, a three volume work (1910, 1912, 1913) by two highly respected thinkers offering a unifying system by which all laws of nature are governed. *PM* captured a popular hope, wish, or urge to bring coherence to the world by reducing it to a single system. This sort of wishful thinking did not begin with *PM*; it had existed long before, but now this reductionist position was given an intellectual legitimacy by the existence of *PM*. The *PM* enterprise might or might not be mathematically or philosophically valid, but as a guide to education it is counterproductive; it shoots for what might be in terms of what might be, not in terms of what is. Whitehead, for instance, writing in 1911, said:

...the first noticeable fact about arithmetic is that it applies to everything, to tastes and to sounds, to apples and to angels, to the ideas of the mind and to the bones of the body. The nature of the things is perfectly indifferent, of all things it is true that two and two make four. Thus we write down as the leading characteristic of mathematics that it deals with properties and ideas which are applicable to things just because they are things, and apart from any particular feelings or emotions, or sensations, in any way connected with them. (Whitehead 1911, p. 101)

This statement is an example of the power of logical thinking and at the same time of abstracting this power. One is struck by the adage, Do what I say, not what I do. In a sense this is a passionate statement of a thoughtful human being in favor of removing passion and emotion from describing what that thoughtful human being does with passion and emotion. He is not talking about how he does mathematics but rather about his goal for mathematics. What are the processes he goes through in this abstracting and denaturing process?

In fact the power of *PM* is not that it is right or wrong but that it contains some important ideas and powerful tools. It brings together in one system divergent ideas of set theory and logic. It serves as an example of a formal system; it helps set the scene for mathematicians to have another way of talking about what they do, in terms of another language, a formal language;[2] and it offers a concrete counterfoil for other mathematical thinkers, such as Poincaré, Brouwer, and Gödel.

Papert sees "the mathematics of the mathematician as profoundly personal" (Papert 1978b, p. 118). His vision of mathematics offers children an instrument by which they can reappropriate what was theirs to begin with but was taken away from them.

Most people feel that they have no "personal" involvement with mathematics, yet as children they constructed it for themselves. Jean Piaget's work on genetic epistemology teaches us that from the first days of life a child is engaged in an enterprise of extracting mathematical knowledge from the intersection of body with environment. The point is that, whether we intend it or not, the teaching of mathematics, as it is traditionally done in our schools, is a process by which we ask the child to forget the natural experience of mathematics in order to learn a new set of rules. (Papert 1978b, p. 118)

We see as central to Piaget's work the recognition of this intellectual conflict and his own refutation of *PM* and logical positivism. Piaget's work stands as a counterexample to *PM*; whether or not his logic is flawless, his data and his analysis demonstrate that there is another point of view that cannot be explained by the *PM* model and that demonstrates that logic is not fundamental but develops over time as children interact with their environment.

Piaget found allies in a group of French mathematicians, known as Nikolas Bourbaki, to provide him with mathematical tools. Bourbaki offered formal support to Piaget's own structuralist vision and directly offered a counterposition to *PM*. Number is not a fundamental idea but is instead constructed; the structures are built up from other structures and, for Piaget, from experiences with the immediate environment and culture. Piaget's genetic epistemology and Bourbaki's structuralist mathematics fit together, but the mathematical tools are still inadequate to describe the dynamic processes by which structures are constructed and debugged.

Papert builds on the work of Piaget and Bourbaki. For Papert, Bourbaki put mathematics back in touch with its genetic (or extralogical) roots. In a genetic theory of mathematics Papert sees that "mathematics can be seen from a perspective which makes its relationship to other human structures more natural" (Papert 1978b, p. 113).

Constructivism and Debugging

Perhaps a key to understanding Papert's constructivism is to note that "debugging" is not just a technique but a powerful idea within constructivism. It is part of the dynamic process of growth and development and is intimately and explicitly part of Papert's mathland. Programs are constructed, tested, and modified. The programs are descriptions—procedural descriptions. In order to know whether a program needs changing requires the programmer to have an image in his or her head of what the program should do, that is, the programmer should have an expectation of some sort of the program's behavior. This might be thought of as a success criterion for the program. The computational idea that objects are constructed by descriptions and that these descriptions can undergo modifications is the essence of debugging and extends itself to thinking about our own learning and teaching methods.

Another important idea in constructivist thinking is decomposability. This notion is the opposite of the formalists' tendency to build hierarchical structures from a few primitives (first-order propositions). The programming term applied to this kind of problem-solving strategy is "bottom-up" programming, in contrast to "top-down" programming associated with structured programming. Papert would ask a fundamental question: Of what are these "primitives" composed? To be sure, they have genetic structures, but what these structures contain is still open to question. It is doubtful, given Piaget's empirical evidence in support of his genetic epistemology, that a set-theoretic definition of number, for example, is a genetic structure. Papert is struck by Warren McCulloch's question: "What is a number, that a man may know it, and a man, that he may know a number?'' (Papert 1965; McCulloch 1965). The formalists' approach of defining number in terms of a logical definition is not in itself an answer to this question. Piaget offers a more useful notion of number; he describes schemas children develop as they discover number in their lives. Bourbaki offered Piaget mathematical supports in the algebraic structures in which number becomes not a primitive idea but something decomposable. Papert extends this to a more dynamic framework—computers—in which processes can be discussed and played with, processes that act on and with numbers.

Programming lends itself to discussions about decomposability. Programs are structures; they are descriptions; and, at least in Logo, they can be used to describe other programs, including themselves. This is so because Logo is procedural. Many programs can exist in the work space at the same time, so long as each has a unique name. Programs can modify programs. Programs can also describe themselves and thus are recursive.

Using Powerful Ideas

An appropriate question to discuss at this point is, What do you do when you do not know something? In school, you probably learned that it is best to wait for an explanation or just go to sleep. In real life, you probably try to form a link with what you already know, or you watch someone else and try to put yourself in his or her place. The point is that you develop a sense of heuristic construction and try something. The turnoff in school is that, like our circle example in BASIC or Pascal, you have to know something about the particular domain before you can do anything. Your intuition, your body movements, even advice are not enough; you have to know a formula. In turtle geometry you do not have to know rules, although you can use them.

And so what Papert is looking for are underlying ideas—powerful ideas—that can be tried out through concrete experiences and that can be built on and thus constructed with. Turtle geometry is one example of an area of mathematics that fosters powerful ideas. Computer science provides rich and varied problem domains that contain more problems than solutions; and even if a solution is known, most likely there is another way to do it.

Perhaps a final point before moving on: Papert does not intend to ''turtleize'' all of geometry (or all of mathematics). For some problems, Cartesian geometry is better. Papert was really looking to create a geometry that would give a child a good early route into geometric thinking. One of his criteria for this was to bring the child into contact with powerful goemetric ideas connected with intuitive thinking.

People and the Computer Culture

There is a social aspect to mathematizing people. Some of the appeal and power of turtle geometry can be traced to the fact that its content interests a wide range of people and that people form different relationships (highly personal ones) with this content. Furthermore, these two facts become apparent to people in the environment as they interact with one another. Then different learning styles, different areas of interest, and different debugging strategies become obvious topics for discussion. As programming projects are developed, implemented, and debugged, ideas about success and failure of the programs are examined in a constructivist way. Idiosyncrasies and bugs of people and programs are discussed. Bugs are either removed, coded around, or turned into features.

How does this happen? When does it happen? A first step in answering questions about the culture which can spring up out of this environment is to talk about actual situations involving people, turtles, and programs. But an important underlying thread is that computational metaphors of the sort Davis finds useful in his own thinking about children's misconceptions are made available to the children and teachers in this mathland for them to use consciously in developing their own learning and teaching strategies.

Programming requires the child to "teach" the computer. The child, in so doing, finds ways to use what the computer is good at in order to help the computer know more and as a result do more for the child. The children themselves can begin to develop teaching strategies and at the same time adopt or at least become aware of specific theories of learning, and they can look at the strategies' shortcomings as well as their potential power in specific situations.

A Discussion of the Computer Culture

To appreciate what the underpinnings of Papert's mathland might be, I discuss various aspects of a possible computer culture built around Logo. This computer culture has a diversity of ingredients, including the following sample list:

1. A computer system: a computer; languages and an operating system; a collection of peripherals

2. Powerful ideas from formal computer science: naming (or assignment); procedures and subprocedures; recursion

3. Powerful ideas from informal computer science: bug and debugging; models and simulations; heuristic methods

4. Symbols and metaphors: seeing programs anthropomorphically; seeing the world procedurally

5. Cultural empathy: reading the signals of people in the culture; understanding the culture shock of newcomers.

Some Ideas from Computer Science

In what follows I discuss some powerful ideas on the assumption that the reader knows the ideas, at least in a formal way. My remarks pick out aspects that are relevant to building a culture and illustrate ways, formal and informal, of thinking about these ideas.

Programming Metaphors

A programming language is used to "talk" to a computer. Within that conversation a program or procedure used to do a task can be developed. The program can be made up of smaller programs or procedures. These subprograms must talk to one another. It helps to visualize these programs as scripts that can be read and carried out by any one of a large population of helpers residing in the machine. These people inside the computer do the work as instructed in the program. A program can sometimes be seen as a script, sometimes as a little person, and sometimes as an army of little people. We can use this metaphor on several levels. We can conjure up these little people whenever we need help. We can simulate them, that is, be them for a while, talk to them, dispose of them! They are eager to help but can do only what we ask. They are literal minded. Each time a procedure is invoked, a new person is called on to carry out its intentions. The same assistant is never seen twice, so his knowledge about the process is static. He knows only what he is told at that particular time.

Anthropomorphizing is helpful in teaching children and is used frequently in different ways in this culture. Our metaphors are based on developing animate attributes of computers and computational ideas. These ideas permeate discussions on bugs and their classification, as well as debugging techniques. A metaphor that runs through all my remarks to children is that we are "teaching the computer" or "teaching the turtle" or "teaching a little person." The procedures are descriptions telling someone how to do something. By creating procedures, you are expanding the Logo language and enriching the computer's knowledge.

The learner builds a set of useful actions out of some already existing set. Procedures turn into subprocedures as they are called on to play different roles. Procedures, whose every subpart is created by a child, take on new dimensions as they are developed and expanded. Although the knowledge of each subpiece is there, the total perception of the procedure changes from a thing made up of pieces of circles)(to a petal (), to a flower). So here is a theory of how knowledge might be acquired; this theory can be discussed with the children.

Children might later discuss what a primitive is, focusing on the Logo primitives, observing which ones they might have built themselves and why the procedures were supplied as Logo primitives. This discussion might involve such issues as bug control, timing, general usage, personal preferences, and systems programming styles. These same considerations play a large role in the design and implementation of the children's programs.

Naming

An important activity in this culture is giving things names so that the user can talk about them or talk to them. The first naming experience is usually teaching Logo a procedure. Some people agonize over names. Others develop tricks quickly. Children from big families seem to use their brothers' and sisters' names. Some use friends' names; others choose apparently random names. Few choose names that describe what the procedure does. If a child asks for suggestions, then I pick a descriptive name. Sometimes we talk about what goes into selecting names. Most children like their personal touch. It is only when their system lets them down, for example, weeks later they do not remember what JOE or JANE does, that they consider more descriptive names. I remember one child who ran out of brothers and sisters and so was stuck for a while until he began to combine the names.

Using names as thinking aids is explored in other ways. We name procedures; we name their inputs, which might be numbers, words, or lists of words. We extend the idea of naming to such concepts as identifying and collecting bug types. We also apply this principle to developing a kind of semantics of program structure.

The Structure of a Procedure

Procedures are named so that we can talk to them and also talk about them. This is an active idea. The procedure has a purpose. It supplies a set of instructions—a script or description—for someone to carry out. It may be for a turtle or it may be necessary to get the help of a little person to read the script and act it out.

In the pedagogy of procedure building we make observations and suggestions about the structure of the procedures. An important first principle is to try to limit the number of jobs a procedure does. The procedure does a job, and even if its name does not reflect it, the role should be identified. This naming process forms part of the meta-activities, which are not directly communicated to Logo. Naming might show up as a comment in the calling procedure or it might show up in the programmer's notes to himself. A naming scheme might begin by identifying the role the procedure plays beyond whether it is a subprocedure or a superprocedure. A set of procedures, which interact in different ways, is built up. After a few such experiences children see some patterns emerge.

For example, some procedures set the scene. They form different "cliche" tasks depending on whether or not they are setting up for turtles. Perhaps the turtle must be in the upper left corner of the screen at a heading of 180 degrees. In a different context, a procedure is needed to set up six variables. Of course, procedures can also be classified as turtle procedures, commands, operations, arithmetic, predicate, list manipulators, counters, search, loops, recursive, iterative, nonterminating, infix, prefix, primitive. Some of these ideas play a more essential pedagogic role than others.

Procedure is a general term applied to commands and operations in the Logo language, irrespective of whether they are primitive or user created. A procedure is a description of how to do something. A command procedure does something for an effect. An operation procedure outputs a value to be used either by another operation or by a command.

We can make up "people" procedures as well as Logo procedures. There are similarities in their structure. In fact, program structure is an interesting part of this culture (not to be confused with "structured programming"). Procedures can have a well-defined structure or can be accumulated patches of actions with circuitous branches. Recursive procedures lead naturally into thinking about structure. Turtle procedures are structured by geometric shapes and changes of state.

Recursive Structure

In what follows I discuss how a recursive procedure might be made.

I start by defining a procedure that performs one action once only:

```
TO HI              <—— title line of procedure
PRINT "HELLO       <—— action
END
```

Running the procedure HI results in Logo responding

```
HELLO
?
```

We have created a procedure and taught the computer a new action. Run HI a few times. If we want HELLO to be printed several times, do we have to say HI each time, that is, HI HI HI? This question leads to the simplest kind of recursion. But before proceeding further, I would play a "people" procedure game. Here is the game. I want you to be a procedure called WOW. It has two instructions: (1) raise your arm, (2) lower your arm. Now remember, when I say WOW, you are to do those two steps.

me	*you*
WOW	raise arm, lower arm
WOW	raise arm, lower arm
WOW	raise arm, lower arm

Okay, now I am going to change WOW. I am adding an instruction. This time I want you to raise your arm, lower your arm, and then tell yourself (out loud) to WOW.

me	*you*
WOW	raise arm, lower arm, say WOW

If you stop here (as some people do), I say, "Hey, you said WOW, why don't you do what you say!" Eventually, you get the idea: Obey commands you give yourself as well as those I give you:

raise arm, lower arm, say WOW
raise arm, lower arm, say WOW

Okay, stop.

Logo can behave in the same way you did. This behavior is called recursion. So now we teach Logo to do the same thing using HI.

```
TO WOW
HI
WOW
END
```

We say

WOW

and Logo responds

```
HELLO
HELLO
HELLO
. . .
```

You stop the procedure by pressing a button on the keyboard. Now I would suggest using little people to trace out what is going on:

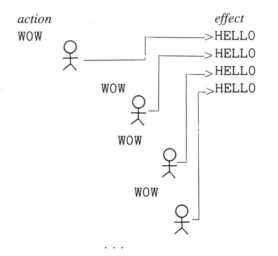

What if you want other words printed on the screen and you want to change your mind whenever you run the print procedure? You need to make a procedure that behaves in the following way:

```
SAY [IT'S A GREAT DAY]
IT'S A GREAT DAY
IT'S A GREAT DAY
IT'S A GREAT DAY
. . .
```

This is easy to do. When we teach SAY to Logo, we indicate that it requires an input, name the input variable, give it to PRINT as its input, and finally pass it on to the next SAY person.

```
TO SAY :MESSAGE      <——— title
PRINT :MESSAGE       <——— action
SAY :MESSAGE         <——— recursion
END
```

Now the title line fulfills a more complicated role. It identifies the inputs by names used in the description of the procedure's task. You could use any word as the variable name; if Logo does not like the word it will inform you. A common bug occurs when you forget to supply the inputs to SAY in the recursion line.

Most often the job of a procedure is to perform some action on an input and then to change the input so that when the task is turned over to a new little person, he receives a different input. For example,

```
COUNTDOWN 3
3
2
1
0
−1
−2 . . .
```

counts down by 1. This is how it does the job:

```
TO COUNTDOWN :NUMBER         <——— title
PRINT :NUMBER                <——— action
COUNTDOWN :NUMBER − 1        <——— recursion and preparation
END
```

Notice that this procedure never stops, but performs its task over and over in an infinite loop. You can tell the procedure to stop by giving it a stop rule. For example, you can tell COUNTDOWN to stop when its input reaches a particular number, such as 1 or 0. Let's call the improved version CD just for ease of reference; in the real world we would keep the old name for the new procedure. The stop rule is expressed as a conditional:

If (something is true) (take this set of actions)

```
TO CD :NUMBER                <——— title
IF :NUMBER < 0 [STOP]        <——— stop rule and actions
```

```
PRINT  :NUMBER                    <—— action
CD  :NUMBER — 1                   <—— recursion and preparation
END
```

Formulating Stop Rules for Recursive Procedures

Many stop rules fall into one of three general categories. These differ in the role played by the procedure's inputs.

1. As in CD the input is a number, and it is used as a *counter*; the procedure stops when the number is less than 1 or reaches zero, for example.

2. The input is *truncated* on each round and eventually becomes empty. The input is either a word or a list that is being taken apart.

3. The third type really includes categories 1 and 2. Here, the procedure stops when the input matches something it is *looking for*, which may be another input, a computed value, or a specific word, list, or number.

In the first instance, possible stop rules might be

```
IF  :NUMBER = 0 [STOP]
IF  :NUMBER < 0 [STOP]
IF  :NUMBER > 0 [STOP]
```

The second type is often of the form

```
IF  EMPTYP :THING ...
IF  EMPTYP BUTFIRST :THING ...
```

The third type is often used in a search or look-for procedure and might be

```
IF  :NUMBER = FIRST :LIST.OF.NUMBERS ...
IF  :THING = [YES] ...
```

The conditional IF can take two or three inputs. Its first input is a predicate. A predicate is an operation whose value is either TRUE or FALSE. If the predicate is true, then the second input, a list of instructions, is carried out. If the predicate is false and there is a third input, which also is a list of instructions, then that list of instructions is carried out.

Starting a Bug Collection

In this culture, collecting bugs is an important activity. The essential idea is that we can classify and talk about bugs; they are not just unpleasant things that are embarrassing. In this culture bugs are beneficial; they help us learn.

In particular we can learn something about ourselves. The message that emerges is that debugging is an enriching experience.

Sometimes bugs are interesting because they cause spectacular things to happen. Sometimes they are interesting because they are subtle—hard to locate and name. Sometimes they are interesting because of what the user must do to get rid of them. Classifying bugs and naming bug types become important activities. Bugs are not unusual things, but sometimes a whole new bug type might be discovered. the user keeps her eyes open for bugs and engages in the art of discovering bugs. Debugging can be fun; it can also be frustrating; it most often leads to new insights into the behavior of people, procedures, and computers.

Here are some examples of bug types. "Slip through" bugs occur when the user has forgotten a stop rule, put it in the wrong place, or checked for the wrong effect; and so the procedure never stops. Another slip through bug occurs when a "truncation" rule is mixed with a "subtraction" rule. "Syntax" bugs can be introduced through simple typing errors such as forgetting to space between words, or through more complicated bugs arising from misspellings or mixed-up input names.

There are also turtle bugs, such as "fitting together" bugs and "attachment" bugs, which have to do with the turtle's starting and stopping states.

Sometimes we need help in recognizing bugs, but starting with the idea of collecting, identifying, naming, classifying what we do find is an excellent beginning.

Remarks on the Culture

Talking about bugs and bug types leads to the development of a metalanguage, a language for talking about programming. This metalanguage can be further embellished and applied to discussions about learning styles and teaching strategies. These ideas provide a way of discussing learning different subjects, which might draw on different skills and attract different kinds of bugs. Thus this computer culture gives rise to a way of talking about learning and teaching generally.

Evaluation

Suppes, Davis, Dwyer, and Papert have fared differently in the area of evaluation. Suppes and Davis have been relatively easy to evaluate. In evaluations of Suppes's or Davis's work, the focus was on whether children's scores on various standardized tests showed statistically significant improvement as a result of the particular treatment. The reason for the simple evaluation is obvious. Both Suppes and Davis offered a set curriculum that was examined in several settings. Dwyer's work, on the other hand, seems harder to evaluate but has somehow managed to evade the issue. It has had its influence without evaluation. BASIC has been introduced without evaluation into regular math classes or has been used in introductory programming courses. Why this is so is an interesting question: It probably has to do with the support from industry and other forces outside education. Papert's work is a different situation. It has been subjected to evaluation, but it does not seem to fit the standard evaluation methods. Indeed, it raises serious questions about the nature of evaluation, in particular, what questions to ask. There are several reasons for this quandary. One reason is that, unlike Suppes or Davis, Papert does not offer a set curriculum in a particular subject area.[3]

The key issue is that Papert is trying to change education in a general way. But such questions as, What is the effect of Logo on children? are so general and subject to almost any interpretation that they surely cannot be answered. For example, in a much-quoted study investigating Logo's effect on children's problem-solving abilities, no significant difference was found in children using Logo as compared with a group of children not using Logo (Pea 1983). However, on reflection, the researchers themselves came to the conclusion that perhaps they were asking the wrong questions (Pea 1984). The range of ways Logo could have its impact is so varied that such vacillation is only to be expected. For Papert, Pea's study was not merely an example of poorly formed questions; rather, it showed a fundamental tendency toward technocentric characteristics. *Technocentrism* is a term Papert derives from Piaget's interpretation of egocentrism.

Egocentrism for Piaget...means that the child has difficulty understanding anything independently of the self.... Technocentrism refers to the tendency to give a similar centrality to a technical object—for example computers or Logo. This tendency shows up in questions like "what is THE effect of THE computer on cognitive development?" or "does Logo work?"...such turns of phrase often betray a tendency to think of "computers" or of "Logo" as agents that act directly on thinking and learning; they betray a tendency to reduce what are really the most important components of educational situations—people and cultures—to a secondary, facilitating role. The context for human development is always a culture, never an isolated technology. In the presence of computers, cultures might change and with them people's ways of learning and thinking. But if you want to understand (or influence) the change, you have to center your attention on the culture—not on the computer. (Papert 1985, p. 54)

Papert's position, however, is frustrating for the average educator who has to make a decision now. The introduction of Logo into schools is just beginning and often occurs under varied and less than ideal conditions. Studies in settings in which pairs or trios of children use Logo once a week for twenty minutes might be different from settings in which children use Logo individually for twenty minutes a day. Studies will also vary with respect to the teachers' backgrounds; settings with supportive and knowledgeable teachers are bound to be different from those with less knowledgeable teachers. Six computers in a classroom is different from two and different from having one computer for every child. Moreover, if you want to know how Logo affects the classroom, then you have to know a lot about the teacher's knowledge. If you want to see what an inexperienced teacher with little Logo knowledge can provide you might first want to know what is possible with an experienced teacher who has deep knowledge about Logo. If you want to know what is possible for some children under certain constraints, then you might want to know what is possible for others under better conditions. You can always compare these experiences to children who are not using Logo or computers.

Against this backdrop of variability the plight of the teacher trying to make a reasonable decision is quite poignant. Indeed the plight is *impossible* so long as the question is posed in its generality. The situation is easier when the question is not about Logo in general but about a particular use. For example, if you want to know whether teachers can use Logo as a "tool for teaching," what teachers do with it, and if they find it a good instrument for teaching, you are led to a different kind of evaluation. You ask teachers. The answers can be statistically significant, but they are not obtained by using standardized tests. Finding answers to such questions might require interviewing teachers, asking them what they think of Logo and if they find it a good instrument for teaching. Studies of this sort are under way (Fire Dog 1984.) Other research questions might require different research techniques. For example, you might be interested in identifying different learning styles that children exhibit in a Logo context. Then you have to depend on intensive observational techniques as well as the collection of transactions made during sessions at the computer. You will also need to have a knowledge of Logo yourself. It would, of course, be helpful to find other contexts in which to look at the same issues or to compare with other findings.

Papert meant for Logo to be integrated into the life of a school. Questions of particular interest are: What can Logo be used for? What can a teacher do with it? and What can a student do with it? Of course, this raises another question: What is *it*?

Unfortunately, some educators trying to convince others to support the introduction of Logo into classrooms are looking for traditional descriptions of its effectiveness. They would like to say that 75% of all children who use

Logo for twenty minutes a week show a 1% rise in their computational skills as measured by the Stanford Achievement Tests. Or that 90% of the children using Logo every day for sixty minutes show a 3% rise in their reading scores. And 80% of the children not using Logo showed no statistically significant improvement in their reading.

The issues raised are not really about Logo. They are about the whole field of education. Look at it this way: On the whole, we delegate responsibility for our children's education to teachers, who dedicate themselves to that task. They follow city, state, and federal guidelines as well as they can. They select textbooks and other materials; they create their own materials; they reach out to the diverse groups of children in their classrooms. At the end of each school year they write reports and provide evaluations in the form of grades, which indicate how each child has performed. These evaluations might reflect the child's overall improvement in the year, the child's performance with respect to the other children, the child's performance on various tests, and so on. The summary evaluation of each child is in the hands of the teacher. Thus, in practice, education relies on the teacher's subjective evaluation. Yet when something new is introduced, this kind of evaluation suddenly seems inadequate.

Papert has said that he was making an instrument for teachers to teach with and that he would like it to be judged as an instrument for teaching in the same way as how teachers decide what poetry to teach or what textbook to use. He would leave it to the professionalism of teachers to make judgments of whether people are learning. You might as well give up on school if you cannot rely on that.

A different class of question that Papert has investigated includes such questions as, What kinds of programming activities do children like? What mathematical ideas do children confront in a Logo computer culture? What programming skills do children acquire easily? What ideas are hard for them? What ideas are hard to talk about? What changes should be made in Logo to help? What other computational objects could be created? What are good bridging activities that relate the computational world to the real world? Is this evaluation?

Beyond Evaluation

Much of Papert's thinking sees Logo as something other than an instrument whose purpose is to help specific learning. There are deeper issues; Papert is especially interested in understanding how people learn. Thus Logo becomes a research instrument. He sees the Logo computer culture as a place in which to interact with learners and to find out more about that process.

Papert envisions Logo as a mathland where children continue to learn as naturally as they did before they went to school. Can other people realize Papert's vision of the computer as an expressive medium, as a carrier of powerful ideas, as an intellectual agent? In his vision, Papert assumes that the computer is a personal, plentiful, and disposable resource in the same way that a pencil is a resource. He sees every child having full access to a computer. For the most part, Logo is not being introduced into schools in that manner. Logo enters children's lives in different ways. Sometimes it is a classroom resource available on one or two machines; sometimes it is a laboratory resource to which children have brief access once a week. Unlike Suppes's systems, Logo is not marketed as an eight- or sixteen- or thirty-two-terminal package to be managed by a trained paraprofessional.

Papert's ideas resonate with the philosophical stance of educators who believe in child-centered environments. For those who translate this approach to mean child-directed activities within the environment, Logo offers them a new opportunity to provide rich mathematical experiences. As already mentioned in discussing Davis, the mathematics reforms of the 1950s and 1960s introduced into schools in the 1970s fell short of the mark. Thus in many open-education classrooms Logo has become another chance. For some mathematics educators, Papert offers a new way to teach the mathematics they have had limited success in teaching before Logo (Leron 1985; Hoyles 1985). The mathematics Papert sees as important might be intangible for others who want to replace the elementary school mathematics curriculum with a new curriculum whose inputs and outputs can be described in minute detail.

For many people, Logo is a programming language replacing BASIC in elementary schools. It is easy to separate Logo the language from Logo the culture. On the other hand, Logo-the-culture lends itself to reinterpretation. Often Piagetian learning à la Papert is interpreted to mean that children do not need help from experts that exploring Logo without human intervention of an expert is sufficient. This was not Papert's intention. Logo provides an environment and culture in which expert and novice can find common ground to discuss their research and the bugs they encounter. They can discuss what they do not understand and what knowledge they need to build on. Papert has never suggested that computers replace people. Rather he has been the champion of the computer as an intellectual agent to extend people's understanding.

Papert believes that changes in children's learning are demonstrable not through testing different pieces of curricula but by looking at the whole child and the whole classroom. Papert's style of research is in the psychological tradition of Piaget. To find out what children think, sit down with them and ask them. Talk to them in an interesting context in which they can give their opinions and their theories backing up those opinions. If you want to know whether Logo is a good instrument for teaching, it follows that you talk to teachers and find out how they use Logo to carry out a personal style of teaching or to enhance their teaching. How do we measure this learning and teaching experience, and how do we talk about it? One way is through intensive case studies of both individual children who have had good learning experiences and teachers who have used Logo over a long period of time. Another way is by looking at the number of teachers who have adopted Logo in their practice. Forty percent of American schools have Logo.

Some Concluding Remarks

Papert's reforms of mathematics education take a different direction and go deeper than the reforms attempted in the 1960s by either Suppes or Davis, although those reforms set the groundwork for Papert's ideas. Those reforms were insufficient. Whether set-theoretic ideas ought to be the basis of mathematics education or whether signed numbers, fractions, variables, and algebraic notation should be introduced in the early grades—these are not the real issues for Papert. These approaches do not present mathematics as an important and useful topic of study to children. They do not return mathematics to its genetic roots.

As adults, whether we are educators, psychologists, philosophers, mathematicians, or parents, we have our own views of what mathematics is, and talking *about* what ideas in mathematics seem important to us is an activity that tends to give a different presentation of mathematics than a blow by blow description of what we do when we are actually engaged in doing mathematics, acting as mathematicians, confronting a problem, and trying to find a satisfactory solution.

What is the Curriculum?

It is this process of actually doing mathematics that is at the core of Papert's mathematics curriculum. What are the "big" ideas that enhance mathematical thinking? How can these ideas be talked about and made functional so that they become tools leading to the construction of other powerful tools? The computer offers itself as a potential instrument for elucidating some of the "big" ideas in mathematics by providing ways to talk about the issues and by offering ways of constructing tools. The computer plays a dual role. It offers itself as an interactive dynamic programming environment in which the programmer concentrates on expressing ideas, and it becomes an instrument for the study of intelligence. How can the programmer make the computer smarter?

The computer becomes a dynamic mathematical being. Moreover, it can be shaped by people to assume different attributes. Papert as a constructivist, seeks to delineate constructions that might lead to other constructions. The dynamic, changing, personal involvement of doing mathematics is captured, and this feeling is part of the culture. These intellectual attributes of computers might not be immediately obvious to everyone. Papert's research effort has been toward making computing environments that are accessible and in which powerful ideas of computer science serve as intellectual building blocks.

Who Will Teach Teachers?
A central problem is how Papert's ideas will be communicated to teachers and children. Who will teach the new professionals, people equipped to live and utilize the computer presence within a humanistic tradition? Papert sees a need for a "new area of study, research and social action." He calls this new field humanistic computer studies. He has proposed the creation of university centers of excellence. These centers would serve a twofold purpose:

as research environments they will allow more systematic, flexible and far-reaching experiments than are now being carried out anywhere; as teaching environments they will educate a nucleus of a professional circle and develop a model teaching program for widespread use as the demand for these professionals becomes so immediate that every college and university will be under pressure to introduce courses in this or related areas....

The most important role of these centers of excellence, and the one which makes their creation particularly urgent, is to help shape the intellectual personality of the new field. In my vision of this field its professionals will need special combinations of competences. Apart from a foundation in scientific knowledge and technological skill they will need high degrees of psychological sensitivity and 'artistic' imagination. For the ones who will make the greatest social contribution will be those who know how to mold the computer into forms which people will love to use and in ways which will lead them on to enrichment and enhancement. To do this effectively one surely needs science-based insight into cognitive and affective psychology. But one also needs a well honed sense of poetics, of how to make that which will resonate with other people's dreams and desires. (Papert 1977a, pp. 6–7)

6

Trends in Practice

Previous sections of this book have explored theoretical foundations of the computer as an interactive textbook or as an expressive medium. Within these two streams of activity the computer makes different demands on human teachers. The role that teachers play might be different from the one envisioned by the designer. For example, the designer of the environment might have imagined that the computer would replace and ignore the human teacher, whereas the teacher might want to become involved with computational ideas and their implications for learning and teaching. In contrast, the designer might have placed greater demands on the human teacher to be an active learner, to pick up on a new and different learning tool, and to adapt the new tool to old subjects; but the teacher might want to remain outside of the experience and let the child's interaction with the computer be guided by the computer or by the child's curiosity. Thus environments developed in the laboratory under the care of experienced researchers might look different when introduced into settings outside of the laboratory.

Often, in adapting research ideas into practice, changes occur. Whether or not these changes enrich the learning environment depends on several factors. Perhaps, the most important factor in this process is the teacher's attitude. It is possible to imagine that negative attitudes could be positive. In a setting in which students already feel alienated from the learning process, introducing a new learning environment that is looked on with great suspicion by the teacher might have a positive effect on the child's learning. On the other hand, the teacher's understanding and involvement with the new learning environment might be the key factor influencing its effectiveness.

One way to give teachers a foothold into the computer's potential is to share with them the knowlege that there are different roles for computers and teachers and students. Furthermore, in the process of seeking out the underlying assumptions expressed in the educational materials offered for these computers, teachers can sharpen their own roles. Unfortunately, in practice, teachers are seldom given the opportunity to explore new ideas and new materials. Often these new, different, potentially powerful instruments for learning and teaching are given to teachers as if they were well understood and part of each person's teaching strategies. Thus in schools new problems emerge. The problems are a complex mix of introducing new technology, new ideas, and old curricula into classrooms when there are a short supply of the materials themselves (both hardware and software) and a lack of expertise in how to use them.

Although people believe that the computer can make a significant difference in the learning process, there is no sharply defined image of how this will happen. In the business world, Visicalc and its imitators, which turn the computer into a flexible spreadsheet, have influenced the way people function. The computer has not yet revolutionized the way learning takes place. Nonetheless, there is building pressure to provide children with computers in their everyday learning experiences. The ways that this potential will be realized depends on many factors, from research and development to public perceptions of practical applications.

In this chapter I would like to explore some of the popular concerns about the computer's presence in education. I do this by discussing research issues arising from the images of the computer-as-textbook and the computer-as-expressive-medium.

Computer Time: School versus Home Computing

The computer as an active agent in our daily lives is an accepted reality. Who uses the computer, when it is used, and how it is used are unsettled questions. In many workplaces each employee has his or her own workstation, either as a link to a time-shared computer or as a self-contained unit. In education, and especially in elementary education, the computer's role is unclear. The number of computers and the amount of time teachers or students are allocated varies enormously.

For the situations discussed in this essay, children were given their own terminals or workstations. In Suppes's research, students were given ten to twenty minutes per day per subject. In the Davis research, children were given at least half an hour per day to work individually or, perhaps, with another child. For Dwyer and Papert, children had access to computers for at least a half-hour per session several times a week. Thus in all four of these studies the computer was thought of as an individual resource available on a daily basis.

Papert himself has been a vocal proponent of giving every child his own computer both at home and at school. His metaphor of computer-as-pencil was meant to be taken in several ways. The computer would be pervasive;

the computer would be an at-hand instrument for any number of tasks; the computer would be so inexpensive as to be considered a disposable material rather than a costly piece of equipment. When Papert first proposed this in the early 1970s, the idea seemed farfetched. Within the last couple of years we have seen a dramatic change in the pricing of computers and the acceptance of them in homes, making the idea much more practical. The new separator might be the difference between children whose parents buy them a computer and children who have access to computers only in school.

The underlying question is, How much time is needed to make a difference in children's intellectual development? This question leads to a key issue: Will children in homes without computers be educationally deprived, or will their contact with computers in school make up for the lack of computer contact at home? A study (Giacquinta et al. 1984) on uses of computers in homes found that in families in which children used computers, the children programmed and seldom used commercial educational software. Their schools tended to emphasize programming and their parents were critical of most of the educational software. The study also found that some teachers were resistant to children having computers at home because it gave these children an unfair advantage over children who did not have home access to a computer.

If we look at current practice in schools, we might indeed think that children dependent on schools for their computer experiences will be deprived. They do not have enough computer time to probe, explore, experiment with, or debug programming projects that they might fancy. If a computer is in use five hours a day five days a week, then in a class of twenty-five children, each child can have one hour of computer time per week. That is, if all goes well and if such a tight schedule can be maintained. Thus, if the ratio of computers to children is one to twenty or thirty, then the ways computers will be used in schools will be restricted.

Take, for example, Papert's image of computer-as-pencil. The computer, in his opinion, should be as accessible and replaceable as a pencil. Can you imagine teachers spending their time figuring out how to share one pencil among thirty children? If only one or two children could write, the scheme would become easier! People need time to feel comfortable with the medium, to begin to understand how the computer might be useful, and to begin to take advantage of its usefulness.

In elementary schools in which microcomputers are introduced, we see a growing tendency to maximize this one computer for every thirty children and to not make it seem a deficiency by putting the school's computers in one room, which is then called the computer lab. One study (Becker, November 1984) found that computers in labs were used for more things and by more people that individual computers in classrooms or libraries.

That same study also found that most students were not given an opportunity to use the computers more than twenty minutes a week. With only brief interactions with the computer, children's experiences with computers must remain superficial and even negative.

The issues of how to share resources and how to provide teachers and children with meaningful intellectual experiences are haunting ones. A study of average children between the ages of eight and thirteen in California public schools with required computer curricula showed that the children held negative attitudes toward computers (Pulos et al. 1985). These children attended weekly computer labs. The study found that children understand computers better if they learn about computers outside of school or if they have friends or mothers using computers. These findings support my concern that a poor introduction to computers as instruments of learning will result in many children either losing interest in computers or feeling alienated from them.

At Johns Hopkins University, Henry Becker has been conducting national surveys of school uses of microcomputers. Data for his first survey (Becker 1983–1984) were collected between December 1982 and May 1983. His information was obtained from over 2000 K-12 schools with concentration on feedback from about 1000 microcomputer-using schools. This national survey attempted to provide a picture of identifiable computing activities.[1] This study documents aspects of the early stages of development of a grass roots movement. With limited resources and almost no training, children and teachers were beginning to use computers in schools across the country, not just in limited high-technology regions.

National Surveys of School Uses of Microcomputers

The goal of Becker's national survey (Becker 1983–1984) was to highlight trends and predict future patterns of computer usage. Unfortunately, the reality of the actual number of computers in schools throughout the United States in early 1983 contrasted sharply with the national enthusiasm for computer usage in schools. For example, at the time of the survey most elementary schools had at most one or two computers. From this fact Becker could see that even if the computers were used all day long with limited access to sixty students per week, it would be difficult to give even these students major exposure. He found that, in a typical elementary school with an enrollment of about 380 students, two computers used all the time gave only about sixty students twenty minutes of computer time a week. That is only 16% of the school's students. Thus, although Becker saw some trends in usage, he could not get more than a superficial idea of how computers might change the learning process.

The study showed that computers were used in the following ways and for the following minutes per week (Becker, June 1983, p. 5):

Time-Per-User for Different Activities of Micro-Users During an Average Week

Activity	Median No. of Minutes of Use Per Week	Percent of Users	
		1–15 Min Per Week	More than 1 Hour
Elementary			
Write Programs, Computer Literacy, etc.	19 min.	49%	04%
Do Drills, Remedial Work, Unspecified Math, Language	13 min.	60%	00.5%
Play "Learning Games," Recreational Games, etc.	12 min.	73%	00.5%
Secondary			
Write Programs, Computer Literacy, etc.	55 min.	18%	44%
Do Drills, Remedial Work, Unspecified Math, Language	17 min.	48%	09%
Play "Learning Games," Recreational Games, etc.	11 min.	56%	09%
Applications: Word Proc., Lab Tool, Data Proc., other uses for Business classes, etc.	30 min.	28%	31%

Note: The secondary grade level includes junior and senior high school. Reprinted by permission.

Because Becker also pointed out that the elementary schools were about two years behind the secondary schools, we might assume that activities in elementary schools in 1985 would include word processing. I would also expect that more work with the computer as textbook would occur. The textbook companies themselves have begun a major effort to develop computer materials to support their textbooks.

Becker found that, as elementary schools obtained more computers, they provided access to more students; whereas when secondary schools obtained more computers they gave more access to the same number of students. Then the average time per user per week at secondary levels was only forty-five minutes, and even with the addition of a few more computers, the increase in time would not be great.

Becker hypothesized that "microcomputers in elementary schools do not function as major ingredients in the teaching of principles and techniques of verbal and mathematical operations, as do other media such as books, chalkboards, and worksheets" (Becker June 1983, p. 8). With students getting no more than fifteen minutes of computer time per week, it does seem unlikely that the time is used in a significant way. Becker also hypothesizes that even drill-and-practice programs can be used as part of computer literacy, rather than subject-matter learning.

Becker's study indicates that few elementary school teachers know how to use computers, that the computers are not used in-depth as teaching tools but rather for computer literacy, that is, giving children an increased understanding of the computer itself. (But to understand computers requires in-depth exploration!)

At the time of the study, about 98% of elementary and secondary school teachers who teach computer programming use BASIC and "5% use FORTRAN, LOGO, and PASCAL" (Becker April 1983, p. 4). I expect that this figure has changed because of the growing popularity of Logo in elementary schools and Pascal in high schools.

[In] about half of the schools with micros, only one or two teachers, at most, are regular users. In a few schools, primarily elementary schools, NO teachers regularly use the school-owned microcomputer with their students. (Becker June 1983, p. 1)

Becker defines *regular users* as "teachers who either use packaged programs such as those for math or language drills or who teach computer programming to students" (Becker June 1983, p. 1). He finds that in the other half of the schools, no more than two teachers are regular users. In this case it is rare to find more than one or two people teaching programming to students; instead the teachers use packages of either learning games or drill-and-practice programs. Becker found that in the majority of schools there was at least one teacher (seldom more than two) who had become a computerist and spent three or more hours per week using the computer to write programs for use with the students.

In elementary schools a computer was used for about two or three hours during the school day, or about eleven hours a week. Thus an elementary school student typically got less than thirty minutes of computer time per week (six minutes per day). A third of the elementary schools reported that users had access for fifteen minutes or less during a given week. His data do not show whether the same students used the computer for fifteen minutes each week. According to Becker's data, only one student in fifty got more than an hour of computer time during a given week. (His data are based on teacher-directed activities, not on free playtime.)

Why Look at Becker's Study?

The general picture that Becker paints is different from the particular experiences individual teachers and researchers report in popular magazines or at computer conferences. We often hear about the activities in a school in which there are two or more computers per classroom.

In Becker's study, teachers seemed to use the computer more for teaching programming than for drill and practice or game playing. One reason might be that the drill-and-practice or learning-game packages cost more money than the programming languages, such as BASIC, which is usually free, or Logo, which is sometimes free. For the next round of school computing activites, the textbook companies are making computer material to accompany their line of textbooks. Thus, instead of using pencil and paper for the exercises at the end of a chapter, the students will use the computer.

Initial findings of Becker's second national survey (1985) show a dramatic change from his 1983–1984 study in the number of computers in schools and the number of teachers involved with computers.

Along with a quadrupling of the number of computers in schools in the last two years has come a tripling of the number of students using them and a tripling of the number of teachers supervising students in their use. In the typical school this past year, about 150 students used computers during the year. And four to five teachers used computers regularly in their teaching practice. (Becker 1985, p. 2)

In a third of the 2300 elementary and secondary schools in this study, there were three to five computer-using teachers per school. In another third, there were six or more who regularly used computers.

Although Becker found that the majority of elementary school teachers still saw computers as instruments for computer-assisted-instruction,[2] a small but increasing number of teachers saw the computer "as a tool for applications—for writing, problem solving, or analyzing data" and not just using them to teach about computers or to give basic skills instruction (Becker 1985, p. 17). He also found:

Again, it seems to be the case that elementary schools are enabling more students to use computers a little bit, but that secondary schools are giving substantial chunks of consecutive daily use to many more students.[3] (Becker 1985, p. 18)

Becker also observed that elementary schools still seemed to lag by about two years secondary schools in computer usage.

Teachers in Elementary Schools

According to the market research firm TALMIS, during the 1984–1985 school year, schools spent $130 million on software and expect to spend at least $150 million in 1985-1986 (*Education Computer News*, September 25, 1985). Thus schools have become more aware of the need to budget for software as well as hardware. The most popular software "teach problem solving or permit students to use computers for word processing, data bases and spread sheets"[4](*Education Computer News*, September 25, 1985).

This raises the issue of teacher preparedness for using computers at all. A study in California (Shavelson et al. 1984) found few expert computer-using teachers in California classrooms. As soon as the teachers became competent, they left the classroom to become computer curriculum coordinators or to take jobs in industry.

Schools of education for teachers are badly in need of plans, visions, and competent computer educators. The move seems to be for staff to retrain themselves from other less popular interest areas. They become familiar with computer techniques but often do not treat the computer as a fundamentally new way of thinking about things. There are the technical mechanisms of creating hardware and software, but there are also the insights into how knowledge is acquired that takes on different possibilities with computers.

Many of the school uses of computers in education, the software and the hardware, the images of how to put the two together, are based on research begun in the 1960s. There were several long-term research projects under investigation in different university settings at that time. Stanford, the University of Illinois, the University of Pittsburgh, and the Massachusetts Institute of Technology are the four university settings that I focus on, but there were others, and even within these institutions there were other approaches under investigation.

Some people think that research on computers and education should be left to industry. Other people think that the kind of research that is needed is evaluation of how teachers are using computers in schools. This kind of research does not take the form of introducing teachers to educational computing activities and then observing how they reinterpret this experience in their own classrooms. Instead the studies tend to look at how computers are used by teachers, who for the most part are inadequately trained and have limited resources.

There is a kind of frenzy with people who question whether teachers should:

1. learn to program and then try to decide what that means;

2. use computers as word processors, calculators, laboratories;

3. use computers for drill and practice to raise test scores;

4. use computers to enhance math, science, and other school subjects;

5. use computers to manage instruction;

6. be software evaluators able to select classroom materials.

Large demands are made with little time set aside for learning and developing. For the most part there is a struggle to relate the crudeness of the hardware and the software to the potentials and the realities. The hardware takes up much space and has many parts connected by cables. The software, for the most part, was written under deadline and has bugs in it. What worked in a laboratory with research teams and large research computers might need to be reconfigured in classrooms, where there is limited expertise.

The fundamental question of how the computer can make a difference in the way children learn, as well as in the content of the school curriculum, needs to be addressed. Does the computer presence call for a new mathematics, science, and English curriculum? Will writing and grammar and other communications skills be transformed when every child has a computer? Will elementary school mathematics need a facelift when the computer is available for calculations? Will science curriculums be renovated as well?

Questions of this sort were probed in the research of the 1960s, at a time before computers were in schools and homes. The transition of these ideas from research settings into school practice is one that needs attention. The number of children and teachers who are newly exposed to the computer's potential opens up entirely new areas of research on uses of computers. Teachers have been asked to reinvent the wheel, to introduce computing activities into their classrooms with inadequate support. They are being asked to do the fundamental research. Although the density of computers to children dramatically affects the implementation of many of these ideas, teachers have been given fewer computers than they need to do their job well and rewardingly. At the same time the teachers have not had enough experience with computers to integrate them comfortably into the daily school events.

There are two aspects. There is the skills development of knowing how to program in BASIC or Logo or how to use a word processing package or how to use some other educational software, including games and simulations. There are also the knowledge and understanding underlying these aspects that tap the computer's potential as a thinking tool and as an instrument of learning. Historically, there has been tension between the skills, or "how to" aspect, and the understanding, or the "why bother" aspect. These aspects are typically dealt with separately. The result of such action is often to denature the subject matter separating the skill from its application and justification. This book is an appeal to bring the two together again. In the next chapter I discuss a learning center for educators where this might happen.

School Computing Activities

Most of the current research and reports deal with how teachers and children are using microcomputers and their currently available software in schools now. The work of the four theorists discussed in this book was carried out on large time-shared computers. The programming languages—BASIC and Logo—have been transported to microcomputers and are considerably popular. The computer-as-textbook, as implemented by Suppes, is offered as a complete system with various clusters of terminals. Suppes has found his market primarily in schools with Title I or other remediation funds for large populations of poor minority students. The transition of his materials from laboratory to school has been the smoothest and has received considerable financial support. The math materials developed by the Davis team for the Plato system are not available commercially.

Data on microcomputers in schools do not include Suppes's work in the statistics. Plato is also not included in the data. Commercial versions of Plato were directed at community colleges, universities, prisons, and adult learning centers. Some attempt is being made to offer services to schools, but these materials are more like those of Suppes than those of Davis.

The 1980s have been years of fast growing interest in computers in schools. Teachers and children have had to work under less than ideal conditions. Often they have too few computers to make real use of the computer as a learning tool and instead end up reducing the experience to a touch or a tap on the keyboard. Sometimes the teachers have been given sudden access to several computers but have had no time to explore the computer themselves. Other times, the teachers know what they would like to do, but do not have the money for the software; then they enter into ethical issues about whether or not they should copy copy-protected material.

Using the computer as a textbook promises some teachers a relief from the pressure of having to learn about computers themselves. For others the image of computer-as-textbook plays into their biggest fear of being replaced eventually by the computer. In reality the microcomputer as textbook often makes great demands on the teachers in order to be used well.

If we look at the way CCC operates or the way CDC operates Plato, we see that, when the computer is used as a textbook, it costs a lot of money for the courseware, the maintenance of the system, and the manager of the environment. These systems, which should be able to run themselves, are marketed with great care and protectiveness. The school buys the company's expertise. The company sends trained paraprofessionals to the site to attend its use.

To learn to program—that is, not to become a programmer but to program—takes time, and it takes computer time as well. Twenty minutes or even a class period a week does not seem adequate for most children.

The arguments that some critics of Logo give is that Logo requires too much of the school's time. The issue of what is an adequate amount of time is coupled with how available the computer is to the children. If children have computers at home, then the way they are used in classroom activities might vary. If enough children have them at home, then maybe the school's computers should be loaned to the children who do not have them at home.

An Image for the Future

In my vision of a future, children will use the computer as an expressive medium. They will communicate in a number of ways: by speech, by typewriter, by touch, by body movement. They will talk to the computer about a number of things from a wide assortment of computer-controlled responsive toys, animated graphic images, interactive stories represented on videodisks, images generated by the computer on the fly, and including historical data on a wide range of subjects, interactive science labs, and so on. The student will be in control, either writing programs to probe different environments or choosing knowledge-based programs to interact with. The computer will become an instrument of commmunication in written word as well as spoken; it becomes a flexible, interactive encyclopedia.

This vision of the computer is for the future and requires a large investment of money and talent. How will anything new and good get done? There is so much money to be made from computers that implications for educational research take on a different meaning. Long-term funding for research on children's thinking or on educational computing is inadequate.

The idea that the computer can be the vehicle for delivering the same educational curricula to a large number of students captures the interest of policymakers and curriculum developers. It leads to the image of the computer as an interactive textbook that can guide and record a student's progress, doing the job that teachers, teacher-training institutions, and educators have not yet been able to do, reaching out to diverse needs in nonhomogeneous environments. The way is to build into the computer knowledge about particular subject areas and knowledge about how students might react to the delivery system. What people have not been able to do, they might now be able to do by putting the same material on the computer. This assumes that there are theories about how learning takes place that support such systems. Some models for this belief have been discussed in chapters 2 through 5. If we look at quality education, we do not see the computer as a replacement for human teachers. We see the computer as a powerful tool. Nonetheless, in the history of computers in education this idea gains the most support in practice and in funds.

Interesting note: Federal funding for educational computing in 1983 was $38 million; in 1968, funding was $30 million (Zucker 1984; House Committee on Science and Technology 1978, p. 9; *Education Computer News*, September 26, 1984). Given the depreciation of the dollar over the years, it is clear that federally funded research on educational computers is at a low point. The lack of planning for the future is noticeable not only by the lack of funds but also by the lack of research projects of the sort discussed in this book.

7

Computer Educators

In chapters 2 through 5 of this book I described four distinct visions of computers in education. Whether the computer is acting as an interactive textbook or as an expressive medium, we have seen that the teacher's role varies in different situations. In this chapter I focus on teachers and their roles. A general issue emerges as to how teachers might learn their practice so as to integrate the computer's potential into their classroom activities. Here I put forth a view that presents one possible route into computing for educators. This path is based on my personal experiences in working with children and teachers. This path has a long history, starting over twenty years ago when I began my collaboration with Seymour Papert.

In my view the computer is an intellectual agent, operating in a culture and reflecting ideas of the culture. Logo, as a programming language, is used as the main means of communication with the computer. But what really guides this culture is the belief that naive as well as sophisticated people should be given access to powerful ideas in a dynamic and concrete way; computers can offer easy access to such ideas as well as models for how to build on them. Furthermore, although there is an accepted and widely held attitude that experience in programming computers is in itself stimulating, enriching, motivating, and valuable in many ways for children, high school students, indeed, everyone, there is a belief that more can be offered. The computer becomes a medium for self-expression and an instrument for one's own intellectual development. This process involves people, machines, and ideas. Each is linked to the others.

Perhaps the major question to be discussed is, How do teachers acquire knowledge about computers that they can put into practice in their daily teaching? Most courses on computers in education take a skills approach, whereby within a semester they provide the students with some of the syntax of a programming language or familiarity with word processing and assorted educational games. In contrast, I talk about what you might do while you take that course or the next one. That is, how you can take advantage of the computer's potential.

For many teachers learning about computers can be frightening. The machine, the keyboard, the floppy diskettes, the typing—all contribute to a kind of bewilderment and tension. I would like to be there to tell you to relax, it's okay. I would like to continue to give you the same advice I give children. I would like to be there to set your computer up so that you are not confronted by the bewildering array of machine parts and wires. But, I can say only that in the future computers will contain a library of information as well as space for personal work. There will be a significant breakthrough in speech recognition so that the computer will understand verbal commands as well as those passed to it from a keyboard. Of course, talking out loud can be a distraction in a classroom. Anyway, that is in the future, and the frustrations of communicating with the computer through a keyboard are momentary and fade away as you gain familiarity.

I emphasize first encounters because first encounters often leave lasting impressions. I want to help make that first experience a positive, almost magical one. Rather than concentrating on the syntax of a language or even a game I want to concentrate on the computer experience itself. I want to provide you with insight into the computer's potential as a powerful personal intellectual agent. I want, therefore, for you to be able to do something interesting that you could not do before using a computer.

Turtle geometry offers a multitude of possibilities to meet these criteria. Although there are other programming domains from which to draw, turtle geometry stands out as the most concrete and obvious. After issuing a few commands to a turtle on a TV screen, you have created a square, a star, a squiggly path showing the turtle's reactions to your commands. You are strongly impressed by the first twenty minutes of your computer experience.

This is the beginning of a remarkable intellectual journey toward mathland and the world of computational ideas. By going from the concrete to the abstract and from the abstract to the concrete, you develop procedures to describe particular actions by studying individual instances of that general behavior. For example, seeing that the process by which the turtle walks in a square path is the same as walking in a triangular path leads to an understanding of the total turtle trip theorem and the POLY procedure.

Computers offer a new opportunity to help teachers to enhance their teaching and understanding of children and to keep schooling from becoming an alienating experience. Whether or not this will happen is unclear. To make it happen, action needs to be taken now to reeducate educators to develop models of what might be possible.

Teacher Preparation

In discussing teacher preparation people tend to focus on what software packages to talk about and whether a teacher should be familiar with Logo, BASIC, or Pascal. In discussions about using computers in schools people tend to extend their concerns to whether computers should be in a laboratory or in individual classrooms. Rarely, do discussions focus on what kinds of learning environments might be developed to introduce educators to a computer culture. Furthermore, the amount of time set aside for teachers to become comfortable and knowledgeable is short. The resulting tendency is to encourage the popular beliefs that (1) educators in general cannot learn to program, and (2) programming as we know it today will disappear in a few years, so why learn about it now? Of course, educators can learn to program as easily as ten-year-olds or they might find it impossible, depending on the kind of programming projects they are engaged in. As for the second objection, it is likely that programming techniques will change, but important ideas in computer science, such as naming, procedurizing, debugging, heuristic methods, and simulations, will not disappear. What is likely to change is the syntax and power of particular programming languages and the domains over which they operate.

Developing programming projects and debugging them can be a rich intellectual experience for teachers and children. In what follows I would like to explore in some depth some ideas about preparing people to work with children and computers. I want to situate this discussion in terms of the question, What does an elementary school computer teacher need to know? I am going to talk about my own experiences. In discussing this question, my strategy is to examine carefully the knowledge I bring to bear on teaching children to program. As a teacher, I see much of my own development as acquiring (1) a repertoire of programming projects that make the power of programming techniques and concepts apparent to beginners, (2) a vocabulary for talking about structured programming, and (3) a sensitivity to the kinds of resistance that keep many adults and children from experimenting with mathematical ideas. This knowledge, much of it tacit and intuitive, developed over many years; I now try to formulate it explicitly.

A Model for Preparing Computer Educators

Becoming comfortable with a computer takes time no matter what the computer is used for. Because this is so, we might as well learn to use the computer in a way that will maximally enhance both our intellectual development and children's. The key to finding such a computer experience is to use a computer in a way that encourages self-expression. For some people this happens by using a spreadsheet program. Others find that using word processing programs gives them a new sense of control over their thinking and their expressiveness. For others, using drawing programs, such as Macpaint on the Macintosh, provides them with a new sense of self-expression that would not have been available to them without the computer. For other people, a different experience is needed. They find a new awareness of themselves as thinkers, theory builders, and logical developers of projects when they learn to program a computer in a domain offering immediate and concrete feedback. This is what happens for many people when they learn to control graphics turtles through the Logo language.

I emphasize people feeling comfortable with a computer because I see that as a key to making computers real intellectual tools for everyone. When you feel comfortable with a computer you can begin to approach it critically and constructively. You can begin to build your own tools or to describe the kinds of things you would like to do with a computer's help.

I imagine the following kind of introductory experience. Imagine that you are taking a one-semester laboratory course. For this course, you might set aside a minimum of six hours a week. In that time you will interact with a computer, Logo, turtle geometry, children, other teachers, and a Logo expert. Part of that time will be spent in the classroom; part of the time will be spent with a computer by yourself, and part of the time will eventually be spent observing and interacting with a child at a computer. Your goal is to prepare yourself for sharing your experiences with children. During the first four weeks of the semester, you work on your own programming projects. As the weeks go by, you find new challenges for yourself and begin to plan introductory experiences for children. In the next four weeks, you apply your knowledge to actual work with a child. I would encourage you to work with one student at a time at the computer. In this intimate process you begin a kind of research project of your own. You have an opportunity to observe and document the child's interactions with the computer as well as your own interactions with the child. You sharpen your observational skills and perhaps become more sensitized to what the child suggests and how he or she suggests debugging strategies or project extensions. In later weeks you might want to work with new students. You might even want to observe students working together, although you will have plenty of time to do so later. You want to focus on you and your role. You want to become familiar with your bugs as well as the child's. You want to think about what suggestions to make that will help the child at critical moments in debugging a procedure.

This involvement is an intensive one. You might keep a journal of your own learning and your teaching experiences as you work with children or as you develop your own projects. Part of the process is to share your experiences with other student teachers, and part of the process is to help you to understand the learning process and to remember your own learning and teaching struggles.

A Model for Introducing People to Computers

When I go into a new teaching situation, I have several models in mind and a willingness to switch from one to another or even diverge from them. My primary goal when I introduce students to computers is for them to do something that they could not have done without a computer but something that they can clearly relate to. I also want to think about a next step: how to build on what happened in the first session in the next and the next. Perhaps flexibility is one of the most powerful ideas in this environment, but being flexible implies having a model to depart from. Thus I have a model in mind of paths a beginner might take in a first session. By now I have worked with hundreds of beginners and so this model has been compiled from many interactions. I have models of both beginning programmers and pathways that beginners might take into the computer culture. Perhaps the following discussion of some of the more apparent learning styles I have observed in this environment might illustrate what I mean.

A Model of Learning Styles

In discussing learning styles I want to emphasize that a computer environment such as Logo, equipped with a powerful, structured language and a dynamic graphics system, provides a solid support for diversity and at the same time draws on a common pool of ideas. I discuss work with turtle geometry because I have had much experience with it and can draw on many examples from my past research. I have accumulated some specific information on learning styles (Solomon 1978; Papert et al. 1979a, 1979b; Watt 1979; Lawler 1980). I mention only three styles of learning here. There are more, but these three come sharply into focus.

First there is the planner, who builds his or her structured programs from the top level down or from the bottom level up but who works from a coherent, formulated plan. Another distinct learning style is that of the macroexplorer, who likes to mess about with subprocedures or building blocks to arrive at a product rather than starting with a specific goal. In this case the learner is intent on exploring the effect of the particular building block, and so the result is open ended. Finally, there are some learners who have to explore their environment on a micro level before they can establish patterns of planning or directed exploration. These students are often the most timid learners, doing such things as assuring themselves that FORWARD 100 is the same as FORWARD 1, FORWARD 9, FORWARD 11, FORWARD 23, and FORWARD 56. Others might exhibit this conservative, gradual exploration by using the same numbers as inputs to FORWARD and RIGHT or by repeating the same commands over and over.

The teaching method I have developed is based on a model of a child who might use, though to different degrees, all three of these learning styles. In an initial session I might try to "plant seeds" for all three. For example, I would encourage a beginning student to drive the turtle around the screen in a series of direct commands with no goal other than to understand the turtle's behavior. But in the same initial session I would suggest some concrete goal, such as making the turtle walk in a square or, perhaps, having placed some squares on the screen, I would ask the child to make the turtle touch them. In this I elicit primarily a microexplorer style with some hint of the planner style.

I facilitate a macroexplorer style by seizing on something interesting the child has just done and suggesting "teaching" it to the computer. Thus I encourage the child to procedurize and thereby turn the turtle meanderings into repeatable processes, procedures, and building blocks and then to use these procedures as subprocedures to create unanticipated designs.

I would encourage children to follow a planner style by asking them to choose a design from a collection built from a subprocedure familiar to the children already or by asking them to make a design of their own and then to develop the procedures and control structure. Being sensitive to at least these styles of learning and their natural intermixing helps to develop strategies for intervention. These styles of learning are exhibited by novices in this environment, regardless of their age.

A Model of Programming

In an environment in which the learner programs a computer, a program can easily become long, complex, labyrinthine—a long list of one instruction after another. I see one of my roles as instructor as encouraging a more intelligible style of programming, a style in which the program is broken in a rational way into intelligible subpieces, but this requires knowledge and experience.

In a first session I would want to convey the following ideas: (1) programming is a process of engaging the computer in conversation using the vocabulary the computer understands; (2) the computer's understanding can be expanded easily; (3) giving words meanings involves describing a procedure to the computer and giving it a unique name; (4) procedures created by the programmer can be used like any other of the computer's words and can thus be incorporated into other descriptions (including its own); (5) making procedures entails a process of debugging; and (6) pretending to be the computer or the turtle or a sprite helps in designing and debugging programs.

Thus in a first session a novice might try out the turtle commands FORWARD and RIGHT. Then he or she would make a design, give it a name, enter that name into the computer's active vocabulary, and use that new program in the construction of others. The expert, at the same time, is learning from this experience. He or she is thinking about making explicit through concrete example and advice, the effect of different actions on the turtle with the intention of helping the novice arrive at understanding and independence. Thus the expert has a chance to rethink projects and their subparts and in the process develops new approaches and deeper understanding of him- or herself.

A Model of Learning as Debugging

There is a parallel between the programmer's idea of debugging and my model of how a child develops intellectually, socially, physically, and emotionally. That is, the child has theories and modifies them as new data are accumulated or bugs are encountered through experience and reflection. Children in natural environments outside of school learn in playful ways, for example, playing mommy, playing daddy, playing doctor, playing ball, etc. They learn through imitation, invention, and innovation. And so in this computer environment I build on this process and look for interesting worlds, models, ideas, and projects for novices to explore.

I encourage students to put into action and observe the idea that we learn by trying things out and by considering the results of our actions in making further decisions. Often we find bugs in our thinking or in the way we express our thoughts. We develop a vocabulary by which we can talk to one another about bugs; we learn to use the tools built into the computer system and to construct our own tools. The process of debugging becomes a fundamental activity in this environment not only with regard to computer programs but also with our strategies in our other activities.

These interchanges between people and people and between people and machines are part of the activities in the environment. They are evolving experiences, and the conversations themselves are subject to a debugging process.

A Model of Mathematics

This discussion focuses on projects in turtle geometry. Turtle geometry allows the creation of graphic designs in a way that quickly reveals relationships between aesthetics and mathematics. These relationships may be a little surprising. Often simple looking objects are a result of complicated processes, whereas complex objects frequently result from simple procedures. One goal of my teaching is to capitalize on opportunities that allow children to encounter an (almost inevitably interesting) relationship between aesthetics and mathematics. The following turtle geometry projects will serve as illustrations.

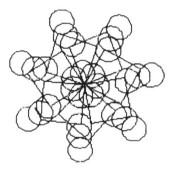

Figure 7.1
The FLOWER Project.

The FLOWER project (figure 7.1) was originated by six-year-old Esther. FLOWER is made from CB. CB, in turn, is made from BALLOON (figure 7.2). To illustrate how BALLOON is used to make CB, let's assume the turtle is in the following starting state, with its nose in the direction of compass heading 0 (figure 7.3).

After BALLOON is run, the turtle's heading is 90 degrees to the right of its initial heading. By running BALLOON again and again, we can see the turtle following the same behavior as in making a square (figure 7.4).

The turtle turns through 360 degrees before coming back to its starting heading, and because it moved the same amount between each rotation, it also returned to its starting position.

FLOWER is made by running CB, turning the turtle 51 degrees, and then repeating these two actions six more times. Why 51 degrees? Well, Esther just happened to pick that number. Why did 51 have that effect on CB? The answer lies in the fact that turning 51 degrees seven times results in a total turning of 357 degrees, which is very close to a complete rotation of 360

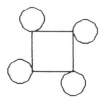

Figure 7.2
BALLOON, from which FLOWER is derived.

Figure 7.3
Starting State.

 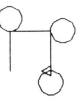 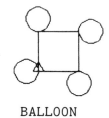

BALLOON   BALLOON   BALLOON   BALLOON

Figure 7.4
Example of how BALLOON is made from CB.

degrees. In this situation Esther was satisfied; for her purposes the design was complete.

A more interesting question is, How did Esther know to probe the turtle environment in this way? She knew certain facts about turtles and turtle-directed procedures which she had gained from her experiences with the turtle (Solomon 1976b). For example, if the turtle draws something and does not return to its starting state, repeat the procedure. Something interesting will happen, and eventually the turtle will come back to where it was initially. On the other hand, if the turtle does return to its starting state when it makes a design, then change the turtle's heading and run the program again. In other words, Esther did not need the expert's knowledge about the power of 360 degrees; rather what she needed was the idea of the total turtle trip, which, translated into intuitive knowledge, told her to keep repeating an action until the turtle returned to its starting state. Esther's learning style in this project and many others was that of a macroexplorer.

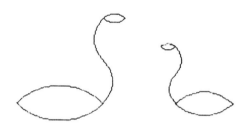

Figure 7.5
The SWAN project.

The SWAN project (figure 7.5) was initiated by Martha, a sixth grader. She attacked this project as a planner. She worked on the project for many hours.[1] In a sense her final rendition was arrived at through exploration, but her overall strategy was always worked out beforehand. Her final scenario consisted of two swans facing one another. One was the mother who waited for the baby swan to swim toward her.

The swan is made up of clearly identifiable parts (figure 7.6). These parts, in turn are made up of either a left arc or a right arc (figure 7.7). The project builds on the total turtle trip idea to make HEAD and BODY, but the control structure that puts all the pieces together is complicated, much more so than in FLOWER, and thus might involve several days of concentrated work in order to debug all the pieces and put them together.

Martha's project also involved constructing two swan procedures, one that caused the swan to look to the left and the other to the right. Furthermore, her procedures could make different sized swans. Thus Martha ex-

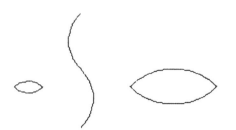

HEAD   NECK   BODY

Figure 7.6
The parts of SWAN.

ARCLEFT   or   ARCRIGHT

Figure 7.7
The two arcs (right and left) that make up the head, neck, and body of SWAN.

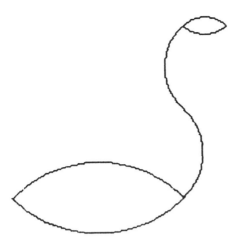

Figure 7.8
SWAN 100, an example of scaling.

hibited a deep understanding of scaling, of relationships of the parts to the whole. For example, Martha could invoke her procedure by saying SWAN 100 (figure 7.8). BODY would be made of pieces of a circle (arcs), that had a width of 100 steps (diameter). NECK would be made from parts of a circle half that size, 50. And, finally, HEAD would be made from circle pieces with a diameter of 25. Martha used both intuitive and formal knowledge about turtle geometry in the execution of this project.

The BEAR project (figure 7.9) was initiated by Lisa, an eleven-year-old from an inner city school neighboring MIT. But BEAR and its derivatives have been developed and embellished by ten-year-olds, six-year-olds, and adults. Lisa had evinced a microexplorer style of learning in her previous turtle geometry work. This project encouraged a macroexplorer approach. Its building blocks are circles, and it grew out of her explorations with circles.

This project is somewhere between the other two (FLOWER and SWAN) in specific geometric knowledge. It illustrates more clearly than the other two that there are many ways of arriving at a particular goal. Picking a starting state for the turtle influences the construction of the program. Whether the job is thought of in terms of subprograms (subprocedures) or whether the design is tacked to the graphics screen (in fact or fantasy) and the turtle is made to trace the path etched on paper has important consequences in how the project is developed. If the design is to be taught to the turtle by break-

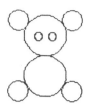

Figure 7.9
The BEAR project.

ing it up into parts, then the programmer has to decide what building blocks are needed.

The bear has several interesting features. It is made entirely of circles. The head and the body are identical. The project is easily changed to focus only on the head or to create with minor modifications a different animal (figure 7.10). The project has appeal to children and adults. Circles have properties that arcs do not: They are closed figures and multiply symmetric; they are good building blocks for the imagination; they are suggestive of realizable and unique designs that satisfy aesthetic and mathematical criteria for a wide variety of tastes. The project is simplified by having powerful building blocks, such as variable-sized circle programs. If the programmer builds on the symmetric character of the head or body in order to attach ears or feet, then the project is further simplified. The same technique works for eyes, nose, mouth, tail, etc.

Remarks on Turtle Geometry and Other Activities

Turtle geometry is but one part of the Logo computer culture. There are other areas of activity that have been explored and many more waiting to be explored. But turtle geometry serves to illustrate key characteristics of the culture, especially the idea of exploring an environment and the objects in it by manipulating them through a complex of interactions based on procedural descriptions and by elaborating the descriptions through debugging—testing procedures in real situations, getting concrete feedback on these actions, and then adjusting the initial descriptions to take these results into account. The process of procedural description and debugging might be seen as a dynamic process of assimilation and accommodation, of making theories and revising them as a result of experience and knowledge, but doing this playfully as an enjoyable activity involving one's whole self.

Sharing in this process is a self-empowering experience for all participants. A different way of looking at learning and teaching emerges, one

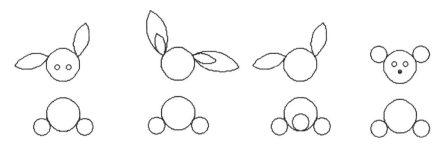

Figure 7.10
BEAR can easily be changed to create a new animal.

that is based on the Piagetian idea that even young children have theories, although they might be incomplete. Thus teaching and learning are not a process of being wrong or right but rather one of debugging. Learning and teaching are seen as a process of developing debugging aids as knowledge gaps are discovered and filled in. The learner becomes an active participant and often takes on the role of teacher. The teacher is not an infallible object in this universe but rather a mentor or guide providing good models to emulate and modify.

Discovery Learning in the Logo Culture

Finally, I would like to describe an experience that captured for me the alienation existing in current educational practice for teachers and learners as they engage in school mathematics. From 1970 to 1971 I was working with a group of fourteen fifth graders chosen because they fell into the "average range" on standardized test or on school performance records. The children were the first group to participate in a year-long class using turtles. They initially had to share one mechanical turtle. It was a big, yellow, slow-moving cannister with a huge light in its front and a thick wire at its rear connecting it to a computer terminal. In the middle of its belly it carried a pen that could be raised or lowered so that it could trace its path on large sheets of drawing paper taped to the floor.

Winter vacation was close at hand. The children were just finishing up their projects. We had discussed the possibility of making a holiday sign with the turtle. There was not enough time before vacation for them to develop letters from scratch and then put them together into words and sentences. Instead I dashed off letters one evening at my terminal at home without a chance to debug the procedures with the turtle. The next day Papert was assisting in the class when the following incident occurred.

Peter was debugging P. It was made up of a straight line $|$ and a half circle $)$ Peter fixed the procedure so that instead of ρ it drew $\bigcap$. Why didn't it close? Where was the bug? Peter was not at all satisfied with the result and wanted our help. His procedure seemed all right. Papert, Peter, and I were on our hands and knees observing the turtle slowly carrying out the instructions. A visiting MIT student walked into the classroom and asked what was going on. I turned to him and stated the problem. Peter looked up in surprise and said: "You mean *you* really don't know how to fix this bug?" He suddenly went into action and got the P to close. Peter told us he thought I had deliberately put bugs into the letter drawing procedures, and so he did what he usually did when he thought he was being tricked by a teacher, he withdrew and refused to play the "discovery" game. The rest of us went back to MIT and discussed the bug. Part of the problem was in the algorithm used to make the half circle, which I promptly fixed by splitting the amount the turtle turns on each round into two separate actions; part of the problem was in the turtle mechanics, involving wheel slippage, something that could not be fixed, only compensated for. But Peter's ingenuity dealt with the bugs once he saw the difficulty as a "real" problem.

This story is not atypical in what it reveals about children's perception of schooling or of their ability to solve problems in original ways. Peter balked at what he sensed was another application of the "discovery method," a trick often used on him, but he jumped at the chance to engage in real discovery. Over and over again children have seen simple, direct solutions to problems for which I see only complexity. So I learn from them. On the other hand, I have often shown them simple and direct paths at times when they see only complexity.

An Image of the Teacher

Out of experiences in this culture a new breed of teacher emerges: This teacher is thoroughly imbued with a coherent computer culture and its language. She knows how to use this language to talk interestingly about things people from outside the culture know and care about. This teacher has a fluent mastery of certain powerful ideas. She is thoroughly familiar with project terrains through which she will guide those who come for "instruction" (but will be given something better!). She has been there often! She knows how to observe people engaged in thinking, learning, puzzling, agonizing, rejoicing .... She knows (and can only know this through experience) when to intervene and when to let the learner struggle. She believes that the key goal for any learner is to improve his image of himself as a learner, as an active intellectual agent.

A Proposal

My intention here has been to provide some ideas for teachers who want to integrate computers into children's everyday learning environments. I suggest a way that individual teachers might educate themselves, making use of courses not really designed for this purpose. At the same time, I foresee the possibility of providing teachers with learning centers, in which this integrated process is the norm.

I hesitate to suggest setting up teacher centers as a way to meet the needs of the future because there are already centers that have been set up to meet teachers' needs. What I have in mind is different in quality. The center I have in mind will give teachers the same rich learning experience as we would like children to have. Each teacher will have access to computers at home as well as in the center. The computer will be an accepted part of their everyday life and thus easily accessible as a debugging aid and intellectual agent. The center will be a place to explore and develop personal styles of teaching and learning. It will demand a deep personal commitment from each of the participating teachers. This learning center will draw on the ideas of Papert and Kay in developing computer environments and also on the work of Suppes, Davis, and Dwyer.

Some Research Areas

Whether the computer will be used to replace teachers and control what children are taught or whether the computer will be used as a teacher's aid and as an individual instrument of learning is an issue that cannot be resolved now. But we must take action now toward working for whichever view we think will enhance children's lives.

The question then becomes, What do we want to learn from computers, and what do we want to learn about computers? If we imagine the computer as an interactive textbook, what dimensions of the textbook do we want to imbue the computer with, and what is possible to do in the next ten years? If we see the computer as an expressive medium, in which the computer as interactive textbook is one dimension, we still must respond to the question, How do we demonstrate the computer's creative potential in a way that can be generalized to different settings? We might see the computer as a bold learning environment capable of dispensing information about a wide range of topics in different teaching styles that we can directly influence through our interactions, changing our roles from teacher to learner back to teacher. The computer with personalities, which can reflect our own needs, serves as an arbiter of knowledge from a variety of sources. This vision is a distant one, and one that needs hard work to build. It is a large group effort needing support, ideas, input from all kinds of educators including teachers, children, computer scientists, and psychologists.

I end this book with some questions. I do not question whether we can set up new learning centers; I know we can. I see centers in which everyone is a learner, a teacher, a theory builder, and a theory tester. In this respect the centers provide a dramatic and perhaps revolutionary change in schooling. Learning is not seen as a passive process in which the teacher (human or computer) pours knowledge into the student's head. The learning process becomes a shared responsibilty among all the participants. But some of the major research questions in these centers are, What are appropriate activities and what kind of knowledge do we expect each to bring to the learning process and take away as well? For example, what kind of mathematical activities do we see children engaged in? Do they really have to become skilled calculators? Does knowing about number and being able to solve problems require calculating dexterity, or is it sufficient to be able to intuit number relationships and use calculating devices for precision and speed?

Will children in this kind of learning environment learn to read and write and do mathematics in a significantly more improved style? Will they be better learners in general? Will they be more aware better prepared citizens? Will what is done in these centers spin off to other environments and thus be reproducible? We need to do research to answer these questions. This center will provide a forum for this research.

Notes

Chapter 2

1. The computer was initially shared with John McCarthy's Artificial Intelligence Laboratory; eventually both laboratories acquired their own computers for research.

2. The original programs were written in ALGOL, the high-level programming language then available on the system. Later the logic programs would be written in LISP, a high-level language that required a large amount of computer workspace but permitted easier and more powerful programming methods.

3. The computer chosen for this purpose was Data General's Nova line. More recently, CCC has been using a 68000 processor in its package.

Chapter 3

1. Historically, this group descends from TICCIT, an unsuccessful rival to Plato as a delivery system. It was difficult to debug and redo the material.

Chapter 5

1. Various versions of Sprite Logo on machines including Texas Instruments' 99/4, the Coleco Adam computers, and the Apple II with a hardware extension have about thirty turtles. All can be commanded to move and turn at the same time. Other computers, such as the Atari 800 and the Commodore 64, have fewer turtles. These turtles take advantage of color graphics and can write in different pen colors. On the Apple Macintosh, some Logo implementations support many turtles in the same window, whereas other versions support many windows, each with its own turtle.

2. We see traces of this tradition in Chomsky's syntactic theory of language.

3. Actually, Papert has been a critic of standardized testing as a way of determining people's intelligence or educational achievement. Although he might agree that standardized tests indicate something about people's perceptions of particular subject areas, he does not think that these tests are a measure of a person's understanding. But, although he vigorously opposes standardized tests and grades, he still expects that children in a Logo computer culture will show improvement in their standardized tests in reading, language arts, and computational skills.

Chapter 6

1. The complete set of six reports were issued during the period from April 1983 to

November 1984. Principals from 2209 public, parochial, and private schools in the sample responded to questionaires and telephone interviews. Additionally, there were 1082 microcomputer-using elementary and secondary schools for which a computer-using teacher responded to an eighteen-page questionaire.

2. More than half of the responding secondary school teachers saw computers used for programming or literacy. In secondary schools there was an increase in the number of teachers from subject areas outside of mathematics and science using computers in their teaching.

3. For example, in elementary schools with over 500 students, a mean number of 280 got access to computers with about 35 having daily access over a period of months. In secondary schools with more than 500 students (usually considerably larger), a mean number of 300 had access over the school year with a mean of 107 having daily access over a period of months.

4. The following software titles had the greatest school penetration in the 1985–86 school year: The Factory, Apple Logo, Apple Writer, Master Type, Microzine, Bank Street Writer, Snooper Troops, PFS:File, Typing Tutor, MECC Elementary Volumes.

Chapter 7

1. Martha later appeared on an educational television program discussing this project.

Bibliography

Abelson, H., and DiSessa, A. 1981. *Turtle Geometry: The Computer as a Medium for Exploring Mathematics*. Cambridge, Mass.: The MIT Press.

Adkins, K., and Hamilton, M. 1975. *Teacher's Handbook for Language Arts 3–6, Issue 3*. Palo Alto, Calif.: Computer Curriculum Corporation.

Adkins, K., Campbell, A., and Newcomer, N. 1978. *Proctor's Handbook for the CCC Instructional System, Issue 5*. Palo Alto, Calif.: Computer Curriculum Corporation.

Ahl, David. 1973. *101 BASIC Computer Games*. Maynard, Mass.: Digital Equipment Corporation. New edition 1978, *BASIC Computer Games*, New York: Workingman's Press.

Alderman, D. L., Appel, L. R., and Murphy, R. T. 1978. *PLATO and TICCIT: An Evaluation of CAI in the Community College*. Princeton, N.J.: Educational Testing Service.

Alpert, D., and Bitzer, D. L. 1970. "Advances in computer-based education." *Science* 167:1582–1590.

Amarel, M., and Swinton, S. 1975. "The introduction of innovative instructional systems: Implementation and program evaluation. I. The practitioner: Selection, training and program evaluation." Paper presented at the Annual Meeting of the American Educational Research Association, Washington, D.C., March.

Amarel, M., and Swinton, S. 1976. "Influences of teachers' conceptions on curriculum implementation in a CAI project." Paper presented at the Annual Meeting of the American Educational Research Association, San Francisco, Calif., April.

Amarel, M. 1978. "Evaluating a new curriculum resource: What are the relevant data?" Paper presented at the Annual Meeting of the American Educational Research Association, Symposium on Evaluating PLATO and TICCIT: Information, Outcomes, and Decisions, Toronto, March.

Becker, H. J. 1983–1984 "School uses of microcomputers 1–6. Reports from a National Survey." 1, April 1983; 2, June 1983; 3, October 1983; 4, February 1984; 5, June 1984; 6, November 1984. Baltimore, Md.: Center for Social Organization of Schools, The Johns Hopkins University.

Becker, H. J. 1985. "The second national survey of instructional uses of school computers: A preliminary report." Paper presented at the World Education Conference on Computers in Education, Center for Social Organization of Schools, The

Johns Hopkins University, Baltimore, Md., July 29-August 2.

Braun, L. 1978. "Microcomputers—Magic for educators." *Personal Computing* 2(1):30–40.

Braun, L. 1980. "Guest editorial: Computers in learning environments, an imperative for the 1980's." *BYTE*, July.

Brown, J. S. 1977. *Diagnostic Models for Procedural Bugs in Basic Mathematics*, Report 3669, ICAI 8. Cambridge, Mass.: Bolt, Beranek and Newman.

Brown, J. S., and Goldstein, I. 1977. "Computers in a Learning Society." Testimony for the House Science and Technology Subcommittee on Domestic and International Planning, Analysis, and Cooperation, October 13.

Bruner, J. 1966. *Towards a Theory of Instruction*. Cambridge, Mass.: Harvard University Press.

Burton, R. R., and Brown, J. S. 1978. *An Investigation of Computer Coaching for Informal Learning Activities*, Report 3914. Cambridge, Mass.: Bolt, Beranek and Newman.

Clement, J., Lochhead, J., and Monk, G. 1981. "Translation difficulties in learning mathematics." *American Mathematical Monthly* 88(4):286–290.

Cohen, D., and Glynn, G. 1974. *Description of Graphing Strand Lessons*. Urbana, Ill.: Univeristy of Illinois, Computer-based Education Research Laboratory.

Critchfield, M. 1979. "Beyond CAI: Computers and personal intellectual tools," *Educational Technology*, October, 18–25.

Davis, R. B. 1963. *A Modern Mathematics Program as It Pertains to the Interrelationship of Mathematical Content, Teaching Methods, and Classroom Atmosphere (The Madison Project)*. Syracuse, N.Y.: Syracuse University.

Davis, R. B. 1964a. *Discovery in Mathematics: A Text for Teachers*. Reading, Mass.: Addison-Wesley.

Davis, R. B. 1964b. "The Madison Project's approach to a theory of instruction." *Journal of Research in Science Teaching* 2:146–162.

Davis, R. B. 1965. *Some Remarks on Learning by Discovery*. Syracuse, N.Y.: Syracuse University, The Madison Project. Also 1984, *Learning Mathematics: The Cognitive Science Approach to Mathematics Education*, Norwood, N. J.: Ablex.

Davis, R. B. 1967a. *Explorations in Mathematics: A Text for Teachers*. Reading, Mass.: Addison-Wesley.

Davis, R. B. 1967b. *A Modern Mathematics Program as It Pertains to the Interrelationship of Mathematical Content, Teaching Methods, and Classroom Atmosphere (The Madison Project)*, 2 vols. Submitted to the Office of Education, US Department of Health, Education and Welfare.

Davis, R. B. 1971–1972. "Observing children's mathematical behavior as a foundation for curriculum planning." *Journal of Children's Mathematical Behavior* 1(1):7–59.

Davis, R. B. 1971–72. "The structure of mathematics and the structure of cognitive development." *Journal of Children's Mathematical Behavior* 1(1):71–79.

Davis, R. B. 1973. "Two special aspects of math labs and individualization: Papert's projects and Piagetian interviews," in *Cognitive Psychology and the Mathematics Laboratory*, R. Lesh (ed.). Columbus, Ohio: Ohio State University, ERIC / SMEC Center.

Davis, R. B. 1974. "What classroom role should the Plato computer system play?" *AFIPS Conference Proceedings* 43. Montrale, N.J.: AFIPS Press.

Davis, R. B. 1975. "Cognitive processes involved in solving simple algebraic equations." *Journal of Children's Mathematical Behavior* 1(3):7–35.

Davis, R. B. 1975. "A second interview with Henry—including some suggested categories of mathematical behavior." *Journal of Children's Mathematical Behavior* 1(3):36–62.

Davis, R. B. 1976a. "The children's mathematics project: The Syracuse / Illinois component" *Journal of Children's Mathematical Behavior*, supp. 1, 32–59.

Davis, R. B. 1976b. "Children's spontaneous mathematical thought." *Journal of Children's Mathematical Behavior*, supp. 1, 60–84.

Davis, R. B. 1976c. "An economically feasible approach to mathematics for gifted children." *Journal of Children's Mathematical Behavior*, supp. 1, 103–158

Davis, R. B. 1976d. "Mathematics for gifted children—The ninth-grade program." *Journal of Children's Mathematical Behavior*, supp. 1, 176–215.

Davis, R. B. 1976e. "Selecting mini-procedures: The conceptualization of errors in thinking about mathematics." *Journal of Children's Mathematical Behavior*, supp. 1, 287–290.

Davis, R. B. 1976f. "Two mysteries explained: The paradigm teaching strategy and 'programmability'." *Journal of Children's Mathematical Behavior*, supp 1, 320–324.

Davis, R. B. 1977. "Elementary school mathematics," in *Demonstration of the PLATO IV Computer-based Education System, Final Report*, G. Slottow (ed.). Urbana, Ill: University of Illinois, Computer-based Education Research Laboratory.

Davis, R. B. 1979. "One view of studying mathematics education research and development in the Soviet Union," in *An Analysis of Mathematics Education in the Union of Soviet Socialist Republics*, by R. B. Davis, T. A. Romberg, S. Rachlin, and M. G. Kantowiski. Columbus, Ohio: Ohio State University, ERIC, Clearinghouse for Science, Mathematics and Environmental Education, 47–86.

Davis, R. B. 1980. "Cognitive models of algebraic thought." Paper presented at the Annual Meeting of the American Educational Research Association, Boston, Mass., April.

Davis, R. B. 1984. *Learning Mathematics: The Cognitive Science Approach to Mathematics Education*. Norwood, N.J.: Ablex.

Davis, R. B., and Douglas, J. 1976a. "Environment, habit, self-concept, and approach pathology." *Journal of Children's Mathematical Behavior*, supp. 1, 229–270.

Davis, R. B., and Dugdale, S. 1976b. "The use of micro-assessment in CAI lesson design." *Journal of Children's Mathematical Behavior*, supp. 1, 85–102.

Davis, R. B., and Greenstein, R. 1969. "Jennifer." *New York State Mathematics Teachers Journal* 19(3):94–103.

Davis, R. B., and Grossman, R. 1976. "A Piaget task for adults." *Journal of Children's Mathematical Behavior*, supp. 1, 315–319.

Davis, R. B., and McKnight, C. 1976a. "Classroom social setting as a limiting factor on curriculum content." *Journal of Children's Mathematical Behavior*, supp. 1, 216–228.

Davis, R. B., and McKnight, C. 1976b. "Conceptual, heuristic and s-algorithmic approaches in mathematics teaching." *Journal of Children's Mathematical Behavior*, supp. 1, 271–286.

Davis, R. B., and McKnight, C. 1976b. "Naive theories of perception." *Journal of Children's Mathematical Behavior*, supp. 1, 291–314.

Davis, R. B., Jockusch, E., and McKnight, C. 1978. "Cognitive processes in learning algebra." *Journal of Children's Mathematical Behavior* 2(1):10–320.

Davis, R. B., and McKnight, C. 1979. "Modeling the processes of mathematical thinking." *Journal of Children's Mathematical Behavior* 2(1):91–113.

Davis, R. B., McKnight, C., Parker, P., and Elrick, D. 1979. "Analysis of student answers to signed number arithmetic problems." *Journal of Children's Mathematical Behavior* 2(1):114–130.

Deken, J. 1982. *The Electronic Cottage*, New York: William Morrow.

Dugdale, S., and Kibbey, D. 1975a. *The Fractions Curriculum, PLATO Elementary School Mathematics Project*. Urbana, Ill.: University of Illinois, Computer-based Education Research Laboratory.

Dugdale, S., and Kibbey, D. 1975b. *Programs from the Skywriting and Spider Web Library: A Sample of Student Work*. Urbana, Ill.: University of Illinois, Computer-based Education Research Laboratory.

Dugdale, S., and Kibbey, D. 1977. *Elementary Mathematics with PLATO*, second edition. Urbana, Ill.: University of Illinois, Computer-based Education Research Laboratory.

Dwyer, T. 1970. "CAI and creativity." *Interface* 4(1).

Dwyer, T. 1971a. "On the importance of complexity in supportive systems for educational computing." *Interface* 5(3):99–105.

Dwyer, T. 1971b. "Some principles for the human use of computers in education." *International Journal of Man-Machine Studies* 3(3).

Dwyer, T. 1971c. "The case for extending BASIC as an educational programming language." *SIGCUE Bulletin* 5(5).

Dwyer, T. 1972. "Teacher/student-authored CAI using the NEWBASIC system." *Communications of the ACM* 15(1):21–28.

Dwyer, T. 1974. "Heuristic strategies for using computers to enrich education." *International Journal of Man-Machine Studies*, 6:137–154. Also published in *The Computer in the School: Tutor, Tool, Tutee*, R. P. Taylor (ed.), New York: Teachers College Press, 1980, 87–103.

Dwyer, T. 1974. "The significance of solo-mode computing for curriculum design." *EDU*, Maynard, Mass: Digital Equipment Corporation, September. Also published in *The Computer in the School: Tutor, Tool, Tutee*, R. P. Taylor (ed.), New York: Teachers College Press, 1980, 104–112.

Dwyer, T. 1975. "Some thoughts on computers and greatness in teaching," in *TOPICS in Instructional Computing*, S. A. Milner (ed.), SIGCUE, vol. 1, 76–80. Also published in *The Computer in the School: Tutor, Tool, Tutee*, R. P. Taylor (ed.), New York: Teachers College Press, 1980, 113–118.

Dwyer, T. 1976a. "The art of education: Blueprint for a renaissance." *Creative Computing* 2(5):46–49.

Dwyer, T. 1976b. "The fundamental problem of computer-enhanced education and some ideas about a solution." *SIGCUE Bulletin* 10(3):15–20. Also published in *The Computer in the School: Tutor, Tool, Tutee*, R. P. Taylor (ed.), New York: Teachers College Press, 1980, 119–125.

Dwyer, T. 1977a. "The eight hour wonder: All about BASIC in one long day, I." *Creative Computing* 3(4).

Dwyer, T. 1977b. "The eight hour wonder: All about BASIC in one long day, II." *Creative Computing* 3(5).

Dwyer, T. 1977c. "The eight hour wonder: All about BASIC in one long day, III." *Creative Computing* 3(6).

Dwyer, T. 1977d. "An extensible model for using technology in education," in *Computers and Communications: Implications for Education,* R. Seidel and M. Rubin (eds.). New York: Academic Press.

Dwyer, T. 1977e. "Personal computers and education: A time for pioneers." *Proc. of West Coast Computer Conference*, Palo Alto, Calif., April.

Dwyer, T. 1978. "The eight hour wonder: All about BASIC in one long day, IV." *Creative Computing* 3(7).

Dwyer, T. 1984. "Take a publisher to lunch," in *Intelligent Schoolhouse. Readings on Computers and Learning*, Dale Peterson (ed.). Reston, Va.: Reston Publishing, 36–41.

Dwyer, T., and Critchfield, M. 1978. *BASIC and the Personal Computer*. Reading, Mass.: Addison-Wesley.

Dwyer, T., and Critchfield, M. 1982. "Multi-computer systems for the support of inventive learning." *Computers and Education* 6:7–12.

Dwyer, T., and Kaufman, M. S. 1973. *A Guided Tour of Computer Programming in BASIC*. Boston, Mass.: Houghton Mifflin.

Dwyer, T., and Sweer, L. 1976. "The cybernetic crayon: A low cost approach to human interaction with color graphics." *BYTE*, December. Also published in *Solo Works*, Newsletter 37, Fall 1976, Pittsburgh, Pa.: University of Pittsburgh, Project Solo.

Education Computer News. September 26, 1984. 1(19):5.

Education Computer News. October 10, 1984. 1(20):5.

Education Computer News. September 11, 1985. 2(19):1–2.

Education Computer News. September 25, 1985. 2(20):10.

Erlwanger, S. 1973. "Benny's conception of rules and answers in IPI mathematics." *Journal of Children's Mathematical Behavior* 1(2):7–26.

Feurzeig, W., and Papert, S. 1968. "Programming languages as a conceptual framework for teaching mathematics." *Proceedings of the NATO Science Con-*

ference on Computers and Learning. Nice, France, May.

Feurzeig, W., Papert, S., Bloom, M., Grant, R., and Solomon, C. 1969. *Programming Languages as a Conceptual Framework for Teaching Mathematics,* Report 1889. Cambridge, Mass.: Bolt, Beranek and Newman.

Fire Dog, P. 1984. "Logo effects in public school classrooms." Paper presented at Logo84, Massachusetts Institute of Technology, Cambridge, June.

Giacquinta, J. B., Ely, M., and Smith-Burke, T. 1984. *Educational Microcomputing at Home: A Comparative Analysis of 20 Families,* Technical Report 1. New York: New York University, Study of Interactive Technologies in Education.

Ginsburg, H. 1975. "Young children's informal knowledge of mathematics." *Journal of Children's Mathematical Behavior* 1(3):63–156.

Ginsburg, H. 1977. *Children's Arithmetic: The Learning Process.* New York: Van Nostrand.

Goldberg, A., and Suppes, P. 1972. "A computer-assisted instruction program for exercises on finding axioms." *Educatonal Studies in Mathematics* 4:429–449.

Goldberg, A., and Suppes, P. 1976. "Computer-assisted instruction in elementary logic at the university level." *Educatonal Studies in Mathematics* 6:447–474.

Goldberg, A. 1984. *Smalltalk-80: The Interactive Programming Environment.* Reading, Mass.: Addison-Wesley.

Goldberg, A., and Robson, R. 1983. *Smalltalk-80: The Language and Its Implementation.* Reading, Mass.: Addison-Wesley.

Gruber, H. E., and Voneche, J. (eds.). 1977. *The Essential Piaget: An Interpretive Reference and Guide.* New York: Basic Books.

Harvey, B. 1982. "Why Logo?" *BYTE,* August, 163–193.

Harvey, B. 1985. *Computer Science Logo Style: Intermediate Programming.* Cambridge, Mass.: The MIT Press.

Higginson, W., "About that rose garden: Remarks on Logo, learning, children and schools." *Pre-proceedings Logo84,* Massachusetts Institute of Technology, Cambridge, 31–37.

Hofstadter, D. 1979. *Gödel, Escher, Bach: An Eternal Golden Braid.* New York: Basic Books.

Holland, P .W., Jamison, D. T., and Ragosta, M. 1976. *Project Report Number 1. Phase I Final Report: Research Design.* Princeton, N.J.: Educational Testing Service.

House Committee on Science and Technology. 1978. *Computers and the Learning Society.* Washington, D.C.: US Government Printing Office, 9.

Hoyles, C. 1985. "Developing a context for Logo in school mathematics." *Logo85: Theoretical Papers.* Cambridge, Mass.: Massachusetts Institute of Technology, 23–42.

Huntington Computer Project, BASIC Simulation Programs, vols. I-VI. 1971. L. Braun, director. Maynard, Mass.: Digital Equipment Corporation.

Kay, Alan. 1972. *A Dynamic Medium for Creative Thought.* Palo Alto, Calif.: Xerox Palo Alto Research Center, Learning Research Group.

Kay, A. 1977. "Microelectronics and the personal computer." *Scientific American*

237(3):230–244.

Kay, A. 1984a. "Computer software." *Scientific American* 251(3):52–59.

Kay, A. 1984b. "Inventing the future," in *The A.I. Business: Commercial Uses of Artificial Intelligence*, P. Winston and K. Prendergast (eds.). Cambridge, Mass.: The MIT Press, 103–112.

Kemeny, J., and Kurtz, T. 1967. *BASIC Programming*. New York: Wiley.

Kemeny, J., and Kurtz, T. 1985. *Back to BASIC: The History, Corruption, and Future of the Language*. Reading, Mass.: Addison-Wesley.

Larsen, I., Markosian, L. Z., Suppes, P. 1978. "Performance models of under-graduate students on computer-assisted instruction in elementary logic." *Instructional Science* 7:15–35.

Lawler, R. 1980. *The Progressive Construction of Mind*, AI Memo 586 and Logo Memo 57. Cambridge, Mass.: Massachusetts Institute of Technology.

Lawler, R., 1985. *Computer Experience and Cognitive Development: A Child's Learning in a Computer Culture*. New York: Wiley.

Lepper, M. R. 1985. "Microcomputers in education: Motivational and social issues." *American Psychologist* 40(1):1–18.

Leron, Uri. 1985. "Some thoughts on Logo 85." *Logo85: Theoretical Papers*. Cambridge, Mass.: Massachusetts Institute of Technology, 43–51.

Loftus, E. F., and Suppes, P. 1972. "Structural variables that determine problem-solving difficulty in computer-assisted instruction." *Journal of Educational Psychology* 63:531–542.

Luehrmann, A. 1980. "Technology in science education," in *The Computer in the School: Tutor, Tool, Tutee*, R. P. Taylor (ed.). New York: Teachers College Press, 149–157.

Luehrmann, A. 1983. *Computer Literacy*. New York: McGraw-Hill.

Luehrmann, A. 1984. "Computer literacy: The what, why, and how," in *Intelligent Schoolhouse: Readings on Computers and Learning*, D. Peterson (ed.). Reston, Va.: Reston Publishing, 53–59.

Mace, S. 1985. "ST targeted as school workstation." *Infoworld,* November 25, 25.

Macken, E., and Suppes, P. 1976. *Evaluation Studies of CCC Elementary-School Curriculums 1971–1975*. CCC Educational Studies 1(1). Palo Alto, Calif.: Computer Curriculum Corporation.

Macken, E., van den Heuvel, R., Suppes, P., and Suppes, T. 1976. *Home-based Education: Needs and Technological Opportunities*. Stanford, Calif.: Stanford University.

McCulloch, W. S. 1965. *Embodiments of Mind*. Cambridge, Mass.: The MIT Press.

Minsky, M. 1970. "Form and content in computer science." *Journal of the ACM* 17(2).

Minsky, M. 1975. "A framework for representing knowledge," in *The Psychology of Computer Vision*, P. Winston (ed.). New York: McGraw-Hill.

Minsky, M. 1979. "Computer science and the representation of knowledge," in *The Computer Age*, M. Dertousos and J. Moses (eds.). Cambridge: The MIT Press, 392–421.

Minsky, M. To be published. *Society of Mind.* New York: Simon and Shuster.

Minsky, M., and Papert, S. 1969. *Perceptrons: An Introduction to Computational Geometry.* Cambridge, Mass.: The MIT Press.

Minsky, M., and Papert, S. 1974. *Artficial Intelligence.* Eugene, Ore.: Oregon University Press.

Murphy, R. T., and Appel, L. R. 1978. "Evaluation of the PLATO IV computer-based education system in the community college." *SIGCUE Bulletin* 12(1):12–28.

Nace, T. 1984. "The Macintosh family tree." *Macworld*, November, 134–141.

Negroponte, N. 1970. "The Sunday painter," in *The Computer Age*, M. Dertousos and J. Moses (eds.). Cambridge: The MIT Press, 21–35.

Newcomer, N. J., Hamilton, M., and Carter, L. C. 1977. *Teacher's Handbook for Reading for Comprehension.* Palo Alto, Calif.: Computer Curriculum Corporation.

Newell, A., and Simon, H. 1972. *Human Problem Solving.* Englewood Cliffs, N.J.: Prentice-Hall.

Norris, W. C. 1977. "Via technology to a new era in education." *Phi Delta Kappan*, February, 451–453.

Papert, S. 1961a. "Centrally produced visual illusions." *Nature* 191:733.

Papert, S. 1961b. "Mathematical models for perceptual learning," in *Fourth London Symposium on Information Theory*, C. Cherry (ed.), 353–363.

Papert, S. 1965. Introduction to *Embodiments of Mind*, by W. S. McCulloch. Cambridge, Mass.: The MIT Press, xiii-xx.

Papert, S. 1970. "The language of children and the language of computers," in *Linguaggi nella societa e nella tecnica.* Milan: Edizioni di Comunita.

Papert, S. 1971a. *A Computer Laboratory for Elementary Schools*, AI Memo 246 and Logo Memo 1. Cambridge, Mass.: Massachusetts Institute of Technology. Also published in *Computers and Automation*, 1975, 21(6).

Papert, S. 1971b. *Teaching Children Thinking*, AI Memo 247 and Logo Memo 2. Cambridge, Mass.: Massachusetts Institute of Technology. Also published in *Proc. of IFIPS Conference on Computers in Education*, Amsterdam; *Bulletin of the Association of Teachers of Mathematics*, 1972, 58; *Programmed Learning and Educational Technology*, 1972, 9(5); *Journal of Structural Language*, 1975, 4(3); in *Contributions to an Educational Technology*, J. Hartley and I. K. Davies (eds.), New York: Nichols Publishing 1978, vol. 2, 270–281; in *The Computer in the School: Tutor, Tool, Tutee*, R. P. Taylor (ed.), New York: Teachers College Press 1980, 161–196.

Papert, S. 1971c. *Teaching Children to Be Mathematicians vs. Teaching about Mathematics,* AI Memo 249 and Logo Memo 4. Cambridge, Mass.: Massachusetts Institute of Technology. Also published in *International Journal Math. Educ. Sci. Technology*, 1972, 3:249–262.

Papert, S. 1972. "On making a theorem for a child." *Proceedings of the ACM Annual Conference.* Montrale, N.J.: AFIPS Press.

Papert, S. 1973a. "Theory of knowledge and complexity: Five lectures," in *Process Models for Psychology.* Rotterdam, The Netherlands: Rotterdam University Press, 1–49.

Papert, S. 1973b. *Uses of Technology to Enhance Education*, AI Memo 298 and Logo Memo 8. Cambridge, Mass.: Massachusetts Institute of Technology.

Papert, S. 1976a. *An Evaluative Study of Modern Technology in Education*, AI Memo 371 and Logo Memo 26. Cambridge, Mass.: Massachusetts Institute of Technology.

Papert, S. 1976b. Un Piaget ou plusier. *Symposium on Genetic Epistemology / Colloque sur l'Equilibration*, Geneva, Switzerland: La Foundation des Archives Jean Piaget, 39–43.

Papert, S. 1976c. *Some Poetic and Social Criteria for Education Design*, AI Memo 373 and Logo Memo 27. Cambridge, Mass.: Massachusetts Institute of Technology.

Papert, S. 1976d. "What is innate and why." *Conference on Ontogenetic and Phylogentic Models*. Paris, France: Editions du Sueil.

Papert, S. 1976e. "Computers and learning." Paper presented at Convocation on Communications, March. Cambridge, Mass.: Masschusetts Institute of Technology.

Papert, S. 1977a. "Computers and people: A concept of a center of excellence in the study, development and applications of personal computer power." Draft notes, November.

Papert, S. 1977b. "Concepts and artificial intelligence," in *Language, Learning and Thought*, J. Macnamara (ed.). New York: Academic Press.

Papert, S. 1977c. "A learning environment for children," in *Computers and Communications: Implications for Education*, R. J. Seidel and M. Rubin (eds.). New York: Academic Press, 271–278.

Papert, S. 1977d. "Testing for propositional logic," in *Language, Learning and Thought*, J. Macnamara (ed.). New York: Academic Press, 289–291.

Papert, S. 1978a. Logo / Smalltalk methods in science education: Moving towards low cost computers. (unpublished)

Papert, S. 1978b. "The mathematical unconscious," in *On Aesthetics in Science*, J. Wechsler (ed.). Cambridge, Mass.: The MIT Press, 105–119.

Papert, S. 1979. "Computers and learning," in *The Computer Age*, M. Dertouzos and J. Moses (eds.). Cambridge: The MIT Press, 73–86.

Papert, S. 1980a. *Mindstorms: Children, Computers and Powerful Ideas*. New York: Basic Books.

Papert, S. 1980b. "New cultures from new technologies." *BYTE*, September, 230–240.

Papert, S. 1980c. "Personal computing and its impact on education," in *The Computer in the School: Tutor, Tool, Tutee*, R. P. Taylor (ed.). New York: Teachers College Press, 197–202.

Papert, S. 1980d. "Redefining childhood: The computer presence as an experiment in developmental psychology." In *Proceedings IFIP*. Amsterdam: North-Holland, 993–998.

Papert, S. 1980e. "The role of artificial intelligence in psychology," in *Language and Learning: The Debate between Jean Piaget and Noam Chomsky*, M. Piatelli-Palmarini (ed.). Cambridge: Harvard University Press, 90–106.

Papert, S. 1984. "Computer as mudpie," in *Intelligent Schoolhouse: Readings on*

Computers and Learning, D. Peterson (ed.). Reston, Va.: Reston Publishing, 17–26.

Papert, S. 1985. "Computer criticism vs. techonocentric thinking." *Logo 85: Theoretical Papers*. Cambridge, Mass.: Massachusetts Institute of Technology, 53–67.

Papert, S., and Goldstein, I. 1977. "Artificial intelligence, language, and the study of knowledge." *Cognitive Science* 1(1).

Papert, S., and Solomon, C. 1970a. Conceptual advances derived from the Muzzey experiment. (unpublished)

Papert, S., and Solomon, C. 1970b. *NIM: A Game Playing Program*, AI Memo 254 and Logo Memo 5. Cambridge, Mass., Massachusetts Institute of Technology. Also published in *Apple Logo*, H. Abelson, New York: BYTE and McGraw-Hill, 1980. Also published in other computer versions of this book.

Papert, S., and Solomon, C. 1971. *Twenty Things to Do with a Computer*, AI Memo 248 and Logo Memo 3. Cambridge, Mass.: Massachusetts Institute of Technology. Also published in *Educational Technology* 12(4), April.

Papert, S., Watt, D., diSessa, A., and Weir, S. 1979a. *Final Report of the Brookline Logo Project, An Assessment and Documentation of a Children's Computer Laboratory, Part II, Project Summary and Data Analysis*, AI Memo 545 and Logo Memo 53. Cambridge, Mass.: Massachusetts Institute of Technology.

Papert, S., Watt, D., diSessa, A., and Weir, S. 1979b. *Final Report of the Brookline Logo Project, An Assessment and Documentation of a Children's Computer Laboratory, Part III, Detailed Profiles of Each Student's Work*, AI Memo 546 and Logo Memo 54. Cambridge, Mass.: Massachusetts Institute of Technology.

Pea, R. D. 1983. *Logo Programming and Problem Solving*, Technical Report 12. New York: Bank Street College of Education, Center for Children and Technology. Also presented at the 1983 Annual Meeting of the American Educational Research Association.

Pea, R. 1984. "Symbol systems and thinking skills: Logo in context," *Pre-proceedings Logo84*. Cambridge, Mass.: Massachusetts Institute of Technology, 55–61.

Peterson, D. (ed.). 1984. *Intelligent Schoolhouse: Readings on Computers and Learning*. Reston, Va.: Reston Publishing.

Piaget, J. 1971. *Psychology and Epistemology: Towards a Theory of Knowledge*. New York: Viking.

Piaget, J. 1973. *To Understand is to Invent: The Future of Education*. New York: Grossman.

Poulsen, G., and Macken, E. 1978. *Evaluation Studies of CCC Elementary Curriculums, 1975–77*. Palo Alto, Calif.: Computer Curriculum Corporation.

Pulos, S., Fisher, S., and Stage, E. 1985. *The Child's Conception of Computers*. Berkeley, Calif.: University of California, Berkeley, Lawrence Hall of Science.

Quality Education Data, Inc. 1984. *Microcomputer Usage in Schools, 1983–84*. Denver, Colo.: Quality Education Data, Inc.

Quality Education Data, Inc. 1985. *Summer Survey 1984*. Denver, Colo.: Quality Education Data, Inc.

Ragosta, M. 1979. *Taking a Long, Hard Look at CAI.* Princeton, N.J.: Educational Testing Service.

Ragosta, M. 1983. "Computer-assisted instruction and compensatory education: A longitudinal analysis." *Machine-Mediated Learning* 1(1):97–127.

Ragosta, M., Holland, P. W., and Jamison, D. T. 1982. *Computer-assisted Instruction and Compensatory Education: The ETS/LAUSD Study, Executive Summary and Policy Implications.* Princeton, N.J.: Educational Testing Service.

Searle, B., and Suppes, P. 1976. "Survey of the instructional use of radio, television, and computers in the United States." *Journal of the Society of Instrument and Control Engineers.*

Searle, B., Friend, J., and Suppes, P. 1977. "The Nicaraguan radio mathematics project," in *Radio for Education and Development: Case Studies*, P. L. Spain, D. T. Jamison, and E. McAnany (eds.). Washington, D.C.: World Bank.

Searle, B., Lorton, Jr., P., and Suppes, P. 1974. "Structural variables affecting CAI performance on arithmetic word problems of disadvantged and deaf students." *Educational Studies in Mathematics* 5:371–384.

Seiler, B. A., and Weaver, C. S. 1976. *Description of PLATO Whole Number Arithmetic Lessons.* Urbana, Ill.: University of Illinois, Computer-based Education Research Laboratory.

Shavelson, R. J., Winkler, J. D., Stasz, C., Feibel, W., Robyn, A. E., and Shaha, S. 1984. *Teaching Mathematics and Science: Patterns of Microcomputer Use*, R-3180-NIE/RC. Santa Monica, Calif.: The Rand Corp.

Siegel, M. A., Bruner, E. C., DiBello, L. V., and Gilpin, M. O. 1977. *Executive Summary—The PLATO Corrections Project: Computer-based Education for Adult Inmates, First Year Report.* Urbana, Ill.: University of Illinois, Computer-based Education Research Laboratory.

Slottow, G., and Propst, F. (eds.). 1977. *Demonstration of the PLATO IV Computer-based Education System, Final Report.* Urbana, Ill: University of Illinois, Computer-based Education Research Laboratory.

Smith, S. G., and Sherwood, B. A. 1976. "Educational uses of the PLATO computer system." *Science* 192:344–352.

Solomon, C. 1976a. *Leading a Child to a Computer Culture*, AI Memo 343 and Logo Memo 20. Cambridge, Mass.: Masschusetts Institute of Technology. Also published in *SIGCUE Bulletin* 8(1)/*SIGCUE TOPICS 2*.

Solomon, C. 1976b. Problem solving in an anthropomorphic computer culture. Master's Thesis, Boston University.

Solomon, C. 1978. "Teaching young children to program in a LOGO turtle computer culture." *SIGCUE Bulletin* 12(3):20–29.

Solomon, C. 1979. "Language in the LOGO Computer Culture," *Proceedings of the National Educational Computing Conference 1979.* Iowa City, Iowa: The University of Iowa, 250–254.

Solomon, C. 1981. *Introduction to Programming through Turtle Graphics.* Montreal, Canada: Logo Computer Systems, Inc.

Solomon, C. 1982. "Introducing Logo to children." *BYTE*, August, 196–208.

Solomon, C. 1984. "Logo: Past and future." *Pre-proceedings Logo84*. Cambridge, Mass.: Massachusetts Institute of Technology, 125–129.

Solomon, C., and Papert, S. 1976. *A Case Study of a Young Child Doing Turtle Graphics in Logo*, AI Memo 375 and Logo Memo 28. Cambridge, Mass.: Massachusetts Institute of Technology. Also published in *Proceedings of the National Computer Conference*.

Solomon, C., Minsky, M., and Harvey B. (eds.). 1985. *LogoWorks: Challenging Programs in Logo*. New York: McGraw-Hill.

Suppes, P. 1957. *Introduction to Logic*. New York: Van Nostrand.

Suppes, P. 1971. "Computer-assisted instruction at Stanford," Technical Report 174. Stanford, Calif.: Stanford University, Institute for Mathematical Studies in the Social Sciences. Also published in *Man and Computer*, Basel: Karger, 1972, 298–330.

Suppes, P. 1972. *Facts and Fantasies of Education*, Technical Report 193. Stanford, Calif.: Stanford University, Institute for Mathematical Studies in the Social Sciences.

Suppes, P. 1974a. "Cognition: A survey," in *Psychology and the Handicapped Child*, J. A. Swets and L. L. Elliott (eds.). Washington, D.C.: US Government Printing Office, 109–126.

Suppes, P. 1974b. "The place of theory in educational research." *Educational Researcher* 3(6):3–10.

Suppes, P. 1974c. "The semantics of children's language." *American Psychologist* 29:103–114.

Suppes, P. 1974d. "A survey of cognition in handicapped children." *Review of Educational Research* 44:145–176.

Suppes, P. 1975a. "From behaviorism to neobehaviorism." *Theory and Decision* 6:269–285.

Suppes, P. 1975b. "Impact of computers on curriculum in the schools and universities," in *Computers in Education*, O. Lecarme and R. Lewis (eds.). Amsterdam: North-Holland, 173–179.

Suppes, P. 1975c. "The school of the future: Technological possiblities," in *The Future of Education: Perspectives on Tomorrow's Schooling*, L. Rubin (ed.). Boston: Allyn and Bacon, 145–157.

Suppes, P. 1977a. *Proctor's Handbook for the A16 Instructional Computer System, Issue 7*. Palo Alto, Calif.: Computer Curriculum Corporation.

Suppes, P. 1977b. "A survey of contemporary learning theories," in *Foundational Problems in the Special Sciences*, R. E. Butts and K. J. J. Hintikka (eds.), Dordrecht: Reidel, 217–239.

Suppes, P. 1978. "A philosopher as psychologist," in *The Psychologists: Autobiographies of Distinguished Living Psychologists*, T. S. Krawiec (ed.). Brandon, Vt.: Clinical Psychology Publishing, 261–288.

Suppes, P. 1980a. "Computer-based mathematics instruction," in *The Computer in the School: Tutor, Tool, Tutee*, R. P. Taylor (ed.). New York: Teachers College Press, 215–230.

Suppes, P. 1980b. "The teacher and computer-assisted instruction," in *The Computer in the School: Tutor, Tool, Tutee*, R. P. Taylor (ed.). New York: Teachers College Press, 231–235.

Suppes, P., and Morningstar, M. 1969. "Computer-assisted instruction." *Science* 166:343–350.

Suppes, P., Fletcher, J. D., and Zanotti, M. 1976. "Models of individual trajectories in computer-assisted-instruction for deaf students." *Journal of Educational Psychology* 68(2):117–127.

Suppes, P., Jerman, M., and Brian, D. 1968. *Computer-Assisted Instruction: Stanford's 1965–66 Arithmetic Program*. New York: Academic Press.

Suppes, P., Smith, R., and Beard, M. 1977. "University-level computer-assisted instruction at Stanford: 1975." *Instructional Science* 6:151–185.

Suppes, P., Macken, E., Gleason, M. M., and Perlman, A. 1977. *Teacher's Handbook for Mathematics Strands, Grades 7 & 8*. Palo Alto, Calif.: Computer Curriculum Corporation.

Suppes, P., Searle, B., Kanz, G., and Martin Clinton, J. P. 1977. *Teacher's Handbook for Mathematics Strands Grades 1–6*, revised edition, version 6. (First edition 1972). Palo Alto, Calif.: Computer Curriculum Corporation.

Swinton, S. S., Amarel, M., and Morgan, J. 1979. *The PLATO Elementary Demonstration Educational Outcome Evaluation: Final Report, November*. (ETS PR-78-11, Revised). Princeton, N.J.: Educational Testing Service.

Watt, D. 1979. "A comparison of the problem solving styles of two students learning Logo: A computer language for children." *Proceedings of the National Educational Computing Conference 1979*. Iowa City, Iowa: The University of Iowa, 255–260.

Whitehead, A. N. 1911. "The nature of mathematics." Reprinted in *Mathematics*, S. Rapport and H. Wright (eds.). New York: New York University Press, 1963, 100–111.

Zucker, A. A. 1984. "Computers in education in the U.S.A," in *Intelligent Schoolhouse: Readings on Computers and Learning*, D. Peterson (ed.). Reston, Va.: Reston Publishing, 289–313.

Index